EDGAR
ALLAN POE

Other titles in *Historical American Biographies*

Historical American Biographies

EDGAR ALLAN POE

Tragic Poet and Master of Mystery

Zachary Kent

Enslow Publishers, Inc.

40 Industrial Road   PO Box 38
Box 398   Aldershot
Berkeley Heights, NJ 07922   Hants GU12 6BP
USA   UK

http://www.enslow.com

Library of Congress Cataloging-in-Publication Data

Kent, Zachary.
    Edgar Allan Poe : tragic poet and master of mystery / Zachary Kent.
      p. cm. — (Historical American biographies)
    Includes bibliographical references and index.
    ISBN 0-7660-1600-5
    1. Poe, Edgar Allan, 1809–1849—Juvenile literature. 2. Authors,
American—19th century—Biography—Juvenile literature. [1. Poe, Edgar
Allan, 1809–1849. 2. Authors, American.] I. Title. II. Series.
PS2631 .K46   2001
818'.309—dc21

                               00-010994

Printed in the United States of America

10 9 8 7 6 5 4 3 2 1

To Our Readers: All Internet Addresses in this book were active and appropriate
at the time we went to press. Any comments or suggestions can be sent by e-mail
to Comments@enslow.com or to the address on the back cover.

Illustration Credits: Enslow Publishers, Inc., pp. 29, 34, 65; Library of
Congress, pp. 8, 10, 15, 17, 20, 23, 27, 33, 41, 44, 49, 53, 55, 63, 69,
77, 83, 91, 92, 102, 108; Zachary Kent, pp. 58, 73.

Cover Illustration: Library of Congress (Inset); Gary Koellhoffer
(Background).

CONTENTS

1

THE MAN IN THE GUTTER

Music from brass bands blared through the air.
Crowds pressed close on street corners to hear
politicians shout speeches. Citizens entered polling
places, eager to cast their votes. On October 3, 1849,
it was election day in Baltimore, Maryland.

On that rainy afternoon, Joseph Walker, a worker
at the Baltimore *Sun* newspaper, hurried along
Lombard Street. He passed near a tavern run by
Cornelius Ryan called Gunner's Hall. It was one of the
polling places in the city. Suddenly, Walker noticed a
man lying at the edge of the sidewalk. The man was
nearly unconscious and dressed in a torn black coat, a
cheap thin shirt, and poorly tailored trousers. He
clutched a walking stick made of hard malacca cane

On October 3, 1849, the city of Baltimore, Maryland, held political elections. It was on that day that writer Edgar Allan Poe was discovered in desperate need of help.

in his hand. Walker stopped short with surprise. He recognized the man. It was the writer Edgar Allan Poe.

Faintly, Poe managed to ask Walker to send for a doctor. Walker helped Poe into the tavern and settled him into a chair. Then, on a sheet of paper, he quickly scribbled a note to Dr. J. E. Snodgrass:

> Baltimore City, Oct 3d, 1849
> Dear Sir, —There is a gentleman, rather the worse for wear, at Ryan's Fourth ward polls, who goes under the [name] of Edgar A. Poe, and who appears in great distress, & he says he is acquainted with you, and I assure you, he is in need of immediate assistance.
> Yours in haste,
> Jos. W. Walker[1]

Cooping Voters

American political parties collected votes any way they could in the 1840s. In Baltimore, poor, wretched men were made drunk with cheap liquor and kept "cooped" in hotel rooms. On election day, they were let out to vote repeatedly at every polling place using fake names. Some scholars believe Edgar Allan Poe fell victim to this practice and was kept drunk and sick in a voting coop.

When Dr. Snodgrass reached the tavern, Poe was unconscious. The doctor loaded Poe's limp body into a carriage and carried him to Baltimore's Washington College Hospital. Nurses undressed Poe and put him in bed.

It was Dr. John J. Moran who examined him. Moran noticed that Poe's arms and legs shook uncontrollably. He was delirious, babbling nonsense and staring at imaginary objects on the walls.

When Poe briefly regained his senses, he was shocked to discover his sorry condition. Dr. Moran recorded that Poe declared, "the best thing his best friend could do would be to blow out his brains with a pistol—that when he beheld his [condition] he was ready to sink in the earth." Dr. Moran remembered, "Shortly after giving expression to these words Mr Poe seemed to doze & I left him for a short time. When I

A view of Baltimore's Washington College Hospital, where Poe spent his last tragic days.

returned I found him in a [crazed condition], resisting the efforts of two nurses to keep him in bed."[2]

During the next three days, Poe remained delirious. He sometimes cried out with groans of despair. The hospital room echoed with the pained sound of his voice. On his fourth night in the hospital, he began wildly calling out a name: "Reynolds!"[3] At five o'clock in the morning on October 7, 1849, the room at last fell quiet. The American poet and short-story writer was dead.

News of Poe's death spread quickly. The *New York Tribune* soon announced, "Edgar Allan Poe is dead. . . . This announcement will startle many, but few will be grieved by it. The poet was known, personally or by reputation, in all this country; . . . but he had few or no friends."[4] The New York *Journal of Commerce* declared, "It will not be denied, even by his enemies, that Mr. Poe was a man of great ability, —and all other [memories] of him will be lost now, and buried with him in the grave. We hope he has found rest, for he needed it."[5]

How was it possible for a writer with such admired talent to die an unhappy, tragic death?

2

THE ORPHAN BOY

I am a Virginian—at least I call myself one," Poe wrote.[1] In fact, he was born in Boston, Massachusetts, on January 19, 1809, in a boardinghouse at 62 Carver Street.

His mother, Eliza Arnold Hopkins Poe, was a charming and skilled English actress. She traveled throughout the eastern United States performing in theaters. One night, young businessman David Poe attended the theater in Norfolk, Virginia, and saw Eliza perform. Poe fell so deeply in love with her that he quit his business and became an actor himself. Although she was married, he wished to stay close to her. In 1806, only six months after the death of her first husband, Charles Hopkins, David Poe married Eliza in Richmond, Virginia. Their first child, Henry,

Also Born in 1809
On February 12, 1809, just three weeks after Poe, another famous American was born. Abraham Lincoln, who would later become the sixteenth president of the United States, was born in a humble log cabin in Hodgenville, Kentucky.

was born in 1807. He was left to live in Baltimore, Maryland, with his Poe grandparents while the actors were on tour. Two years later, Edgar was born in Boston.

The Kindness of Strangers

Eliza and David Poe continued their acting careers. But David Poe was not a skilled actor, and he often drank. One night, he even became too drunk to go on stage. He had a fiery temper, and he and his wife argued increasingly about his drinking. Eliza was pregnant again when she and her husband had a final argument. David Poe abruptly deserted her and vanished forever. It is believed that he died in Norfolk, Virginia, in December 1811.

To provide for her children, Eliza Poe traveled to Richmond, Virginia, to act. She charmed Richmond theater audiences through the summer and fall of 1810. In December of that year, she gave birth to her third child, Rosalie.

Eliza Poe acted for the last time on October 11, 1811. In November, she fell ill. Two-year-old Edgar often stayed at her bedside in her room at the Washington Tavern. He heard her constant choking coughs and saw her agony as she spat up blood. She suffered from tuberculosis, a lung disease that was common in those days.

Several kind Richmond ladies nursed Eliza Poe during her illness. "A singular fashion prevails here this season—it is charity," wrote Richmond plantation owner Samuel Mordecai in a letter to his sister. "Mrs. Poe, who you know is a very handsome woman, happens to be very sick. . . ."[2] Unable to earn money, the sick actress needed whatever help she could get. A notice in the November 29, Richmond *Enquirer* read: "*To the humane heart* On this night, *Mrs. Poe*, lingering on the bed of disease and surrounded by her children, *asks your assistance and asks it perhaps for the last time.*"[3]

On December 8, 1811, Eliza Poe died at the age of twenty-four. The three Poe children suddenly became orphans. Henry Poe remained with his grandparents in Baltimore. A Richmond family called the MacKenzies took baby Rosalie home to care for her. Little Edgar was led by Frances Allan and her husband, John, to their Richmond home. They had an apartment on Capitol Square, above the general store of Ellis & Allan. Frances Allan was known in Richmond as a tender-hearted woman. Her Scottish husband, John Allan, was called quick-tempered. Allan and his partner Charles Ellis were merchants who bought and sold tobacco, grain, farm equipment, and hardware, as well

*Eliza Arnold Hopkins Poe was a skilled actress who charmed theater
audiences throughout the eastern United States. Sadly, she died at the
age of twenty-four and left her son Edgar an orphan.*

as tea and coffee, cloth, wines, and liquor. The two men traded in real estate, horses, and even slaves.

At the Allan home, Frances and her sister Nancy spoiled little Edgar and dressed him in fine clothes. He was a handsome child with dark curls and shining eyes. As he grew older, John Allan sent the boy to school, where he proved to be an excellent student. The Allans, who had no children of their own, soon regarded Edgar Poe as their adopted son, even though they did not legally adopt him. However, they did put the name Allan in the middle of his name, and he became known as Edgar Allan Poe.

The English Schoolboy

In 1815, Ellis & Allan decided to establish a branch office in Great Britain. On June 23, 1815, the Allans and their foster son boarded the sailing ship *Lothair* bound for Liverpool. A thirty-four-day voyage carried the ship across the tossing Atlantic waves. By October 1815, John Allan had established an office in the Bloomsbury section of London.

For two years, young Edgar attended a local boarding school. Then, in September 1818, the nine-year-old boy entered the Reverend John Bransby's Manor House School. The Manor House School was located in the village of Stoke Newington, four miles north of London. Reverend Bransby later recalled, "Edgar Allan was a quick and clever boy and would have been a very good boy if he had not been spoilt by his parents."[4] At the Bransby Manor House School,

A view of Reverend John Bransby's Manor House School. Young Poe attended this English boarding school for two years.

Edgar studied French, Latin, and other subjects for two years.

The Return to Richmond

Unfortunately, the London branch of Ellis & Allan failed to do well. The Allans prepared to return to Richmond. They boarded the ship *Martha* and sailed from Liverpool, England, in June 1820. Edgar greatly enjoyed the voyage and listened carefully when the sailors told fantastic stories of the sea. At last, the *Martha* docked in New York Harbor, and by August 2, 1820, the Allans were back in Richmond. They moved into the Ellis house on the corner of Franklin and Second streets.

For nearly a year, while Allan and Ellis struggled to keep their business going, the two families lived together. Ellis's son, Thomas, became good friends with Edgar. "No boy ever had a greater influence over me than he had," Ellis recalled. "[M]y admiration for him scarcely knew bounds. . . ."[5]

In the summer of 1821, the Allans moved into a rented cottage on Fifth Street. Already Edgar was attending a school run by Joseph H. Clarke. Clarke recalled that young Poe was "a favorite even with those above his years. . . . He had a sensitive and tender heart, and would strain every nerve to oblige a friend."[6] In April 1823, fourteen-year-old Poe entered William Burke's school. During the next two years, he studied Greek, Latin, French, Italian, geography, and grammar.

Poe was also an athlete. Classmate John Preston remembered, "He was a swift runner, a wonderful leaper, and what was more rare, a boxer."[7] One summer day, Poe swam across the James River on a dare. A witness remembered, "Poe did not seem at all fatigued, and walked back to Richmond immediately after the feat."[8]

The Sensitive Young Writer

Even as a teenager, Edgar Allan Poe was trying to imitate his favorite romantic poets. "Not a little of Poe's time, in school and out of it," his classmate John Preston recalled, "was occupied with writing verses.

As we sat together he would show them to me, and even sometimes ask my opinion. . . ."[9]

One of Poe's closest friends was classmate Robert Stanard. Often Poe visited the elegant Stanard home. There, he met Jane Stith Stanard, Robert's mother. She was a graceful woman whose sympathetic nature captured Poe's heart. Sadly, Mrs. Stanard's health soon began to decline. She had developed a brain tumor. On April 28, 1824, she died. Her painful death greatly affected fifteen-year-old Poe. His image of her became his ideal of beauty, and his thoughts of perfect beauty became forever identified with death.

A Change of Fortune

During these years, John Allan's luck failed, until finally Ellis & Allan went out of business. The Allan family faced financial hardship through the winter of 1824. Then Allan's uncle William Galt, one of the

Lafayette Returns

As a brave general in the Revolutionary War from 1777–1783, the French Marquis de Lafayette became an American hero. In 1824, Lafayette revisited the United States, where he received a warm welcome. In October 1824, fifteen-year-old Poe served as a lieutenant in a volunteer militia company called the "Junior Morgan Riflemen." Poe and his friends paraded in Richmond in honor of the old general.

The Marquis de Lafayette (seen here), hero of the American Revolution, visited Richmond in the fall of 1824. Edgar Allan Poe was among the volunteers who marched in Lafayette's honor.

wealthiest men in Virginia, died in March 1825. By a twist of fate, Allan suddenly inherited a vast fortune of several hundred thousand dollars. Allan soon bought an expensive house at the corner of Fifth and Main streets. Poe imagined that he might inherit Allan's great wealth one day.

Unfortunately, however, Poe and Allan did not always get along. A family friend recalled, "Mr. Allan was a good man in his way, but Edgar was not fond of him."[10] For his part, Allan claimed, "The boy possesses not a . . . particle of gratitude for all my care and kindliness toward him."[11]

During 1825, Poe studied to enter the University of Virginia. That same year, he fell in love with Sarah Elmira Royster, his fifteen-year-old neighbor. She was known by her middle name, Elmira. "He was a beautiful boy," Elmira later remembered. "—not very talkative. When he did talk though he was pleasant but his general manner was sad."[12] The two teenagers secretly became engaged.

3

SCHOLAR, SOLDIER, POET, STORY WRITER

The future looked happy for seventeen-year-old Edgar Allan Poe in 1826. He was a Virginia gentleman living a life of luxury. He was engaged to a beautiful girl, and he was about to begin his education at the University of Virginia.

At the University of Virginia

In February 1826, Poe received $110 from John Allan and set out on a two-day stagecoach ride westward. On St. Valentine's Day, he registered at the University of Virginia at Charlottesville. Former United States President Thomas Jefferson had founded the university in 1819. Jefferson had selected the ground, designed the buildings, hired the professors, and had even planned the classes.

A view of the University of Virginia, at Charlottesville. Poe arrived in February 1826, hoping to get a college education.

From the money his foster father had given him, Poe paid the tuition fee of sixty dollars to attend classes. He paid another twenty-five dollars for the rent of his dormitory room at Number 13, West Range. When he opened the door, however, he discovered that the room contained no furniture. He drew more money from his wallet to pay for a bed, a desk, and other furniture. He also had to promise to pay for all his meals. By the end of his very first day at the university, Poe was in debt. He wrote to Allan immediately, but his foster father sent only a fraction of the money he needed.

In class, Poe studied Greek, Latin, French, Spanish, and Italian. Back in his room, he would light a fire, read romantic poetry, and write long letters to

Elmira Royster. On pleasant afternoons, he strolled the university grounds or visited the rooms of his classmates.

Poe rarely had to study hard. His intellect and memory were great. He had to prepare only a few minutes before his classes in order to get the best grades. Sometimes he read his friends stories and poems he had written. One fellow student remembered that Poe had "finely marked features, and eyes dark, liquid and expressive."[1]

Shameful Debts

Many rich young Virginia gentlemen attended the university. Some had brought horses, hunting dogs, and even personal slaves to school with them. The university

Poe and the Presidents

Before his death on July 4, 1826, Thomas Jefferson often invited University of Virginia students to dine with him at his nearby estate, Monticello. It is very likely that Poe met him. Two other former United States presidents also took a personal interest in the university. During examinations in December 1826, Poe and his classmates were tested for two to three hours in each of their subjects by ex-presidents James Madison and James Monroe. Poe passed with high honors in both ancient and modern languages.

was sometimes a wild place, where gambling, drinking, fights, and even duels took place. Poe felt he had to join in the parties. He drank and gambled and bought expensive clothes like his classmates. Before long, he was $2,000 in debt. It was a sum more than twice what a skilled craftsman earned in a year. When John Allan learned of Poe's enormous debts, he was furious. He paid only those debts he considered owed according to the law, and took Poe out of school.[2]

On December 15, 1826, Poe returned to Richmond in disgrace. He called at the Royster house to visit Elmira. But he was told that she was away visiting friends in the country. Poe soon suspected that her father disapproved of him. Mr. Royster surely knew that John Allan was not pleased with his foster son. Before long, Poe was shocked to discover that Elmira had promised to marry another man. Bitter, Poe stayed in his room, working on several sad-spirited poems. The longest of them, "Tamerlane," described the regrets of Tamerlane, the ancient Asian conqueror of Iran, Iraq, Turkey, and Afghanistan. In Poe's version, Tamerlane leaves his childhood sweetheart to pursue his ambition, and as a result, loses her.

The tension between Poe and John Allan mounted until the middle of March 1827. One morning, an argument broke out between the two. They shouted at one another, and Poe finally rushed from the house. Allan soon received a note from him: "My determination is at length taken, to leave your house and [try] to find some place in this world, where I will be treated—not as *you* have treated me—."[3] He asked

Allan only to give him his trunk with his clothes and books and enough money to travel north.

Allan scoffed at the idea of sending him money. The next day, Poe wrote again. "I am in the greatest [need]," he pleaded, "not having tasted food since Yesterday morning. I have no where to sleep at night, but roam about the Streets —I am nearly exhausted."[4] Perhaps his loving foster mother, Frances Allan, sent him some money. On March 24, Poe was able to leave Richmond and make his way north out of Virginia. The end of his education, the loss of his beloved Elmira Royster, his bitter quarrel with John Allan, and his sudden poverty were all terrible blows.

Private Edgar A. Perry

Eighteen-year-old Poe arrived by boat in Boston, Massachusetts, on April 3, 1827. After seven weeks of poverty in Boston, he was desperate for work. He knew that the United States Army was recruiting soldiers to man the forts guarding America's harbors. On May 26, 1827, he joined Battery H of the 1st United States Artillery Regiment, stationed at Fort Independence in Boston Harbor. Being a common soldier was not the kind of work for which a Virginia gentleman was raised. Ashamed to reveal his true identity, he gave his name as Edgar A. Perry. Today, a person eighteen years old is legally an adult. But back then, a person needed to be at least twenty-one to make lawful personal decisions. As a result, Poe lied and gave his age as twenty-two. His pay as a private would be five dollars a month.

Boston Harbor as it looked when Poe arrived in the Massachusetts city in the spring of 1827. In need of money, he soon joined the United States Army as a private.

Now each morning at dawn Poe was awakened by the sound of the bugle. He hurried into line for roll call. Throughout the summer, he trained and drilled. Officers at Fort Independence soon recognized that "Private Perry" was well educated. He was given the duty of company clerk. He wrote letters dictated by the officers and prepared payrolls and attendance records.

In his spare time, Poe continued to write and revise his poems. He had enough by now to make a thin book. In Boston, he found a printer named Calvin Thomas and arranged to have a forty-two-page pamphlet printed. *Tamerlane and Other Poems* was paid for by Poe and published anonymously "By a Bostonian" in July 1827. Few copies were sold, but Poe was proud to call himself a published poet.

Duty at Fort Moultrie and Fort Monroe

In the fall of 1827, Poe's artillery regiment was ordered south to Fort Moultrie on Sullivan's Island in Charleston Harbor, South Carolina. The regiment arrived by boat in Charleston Harbor in November. While on duty at Fort Moultrie, Poe met Dr. Edmund Ravenel, a specialist in biology who lived on the island. Poe spent most of his free time exploring the island with Ravenel, examining shells and searching for unusual insects.

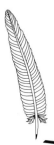

A Collector's Item

Only forty copies of *Tamerlane and Other Poems* were printed, and only twelve copies are known to exist today. David Redden, the head of the book department at Sotheby's auction house, has stated, "It is the rarest printed book in literary America. . . . the first book by one of America's greatest authors."[5] In 1988, an antiques collector was looking through a roadside barn in New Hampshire when he spotted a copy of the rare book in a pile of farming pamphlets. He paid just fifteen dollars for it, and at a Sotheby's auction, it later brought $180,000.

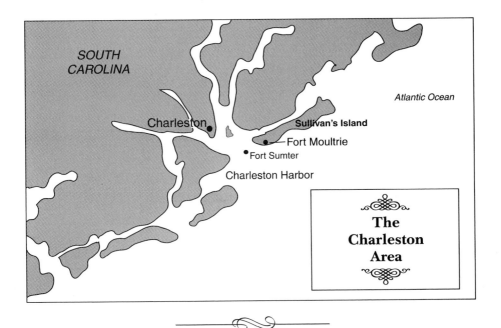

The Charleston Area

As a soldier in the United States Army, Poe served at Fort Moultrie in Charleston Harbor, South Carolina.

In May 1828, Poe became an artificer. An artificer was a soldier who prepared explosive artillery shells. For this dangerous job, his pay was doubled to ten dollars a month.

In time, Poe revealed his desire to become an army officer. He became determined to enter the United States Military Academy at West Point. If he could heal his differences with John Allan, he could obtain his discharge from the army. He needed Allan's help because he was still under twenty-one years of age. On December 1, he wrote to his foster father, declaring that he had changed his careless ways.[6] At about this time, his regiment received orders to transfer to Fort Monroe, Virginia. On December 15, 1828, it arrived by boat at Fort Monroe at the mouth of the James River.

On January 1, 1829, Poe was promoted to sergeant major. It was the highest rank a soldier could reach without becoming an officer. He hardly enjoyed the honor, however. He had learned that his foster mother was deathly ill. Frances Allan died on February 28. Poe received a ten-day leave from the army and arrived in Richmond the evening after the funeral. Remorseful that his wife had died before she could see her boy, John Allan forgave Poe. He agreed to try to help him get an appointment to West Point.

Getting a West Point Appointment

Poe needed to hire a substitute in order to leave the army. He was required to find a man to take his place in the ranks. He knew Sergeant Samuel Graves had just left the army. Poe persuaded Graves to reenlist for a bounty of seventy-five dollars. Poe paid him twenty-five dollars in cash and pledged to pay the rest later.

Having supplied a substitute, Poe was finally released from the service on April 15, 1829. In order to be admitted to West Point, Poe needed to be nominated by his congressman. With Allan's help, he got a letter of recommendation from his congressman, James T. Preston. He also obtained supportive letters from officer friends. John Allan wrote a letter to Secretary of War John Eaton. However, the letter showed no real support of Poe. Allan told Eaton that

Poe was no relation to him, but only a young man in whom he took a casual interest.

Allan gave Poe fifty dollars, and in May 1829, Poe left for a visit to Baltimore, Maryland. Except for his brother, Henry, he had never seen any of his Baltimore relatives before. His grandfather, Major David Poe, had been a Revolutionary War soldier. He had been assistant deputy quartermaster general of the United States Army. His sickly grandmother, widow of Major Poe, still received a pension of $240 a year from the government for her husband's service. Living with her was her widowed daughter, Mrs. Maria Clemm; Maria's two children, eleven-year-old Henry and seven-year-old Virginia; and Edgar's brother, Henry.

Poe was shocked to learn that the family depended so much on the small government pension. He stayed in Baltimore with his poor relatives, reading, writing, and looking for work. In July, he walked forty miles to Washington, D.C. The journey took a day and a half. He went to the War Department and had an interview with Secretary of War Eaton. Eaton politely explained that Poe would have to wait a year for his West Point appointment. With that information, Poe returned by foot to Baltimore.

Al Aaraaf, Tamerlane and Minor Poems

By the fall of 1829, Poe's wallet was almost empty. John Allan resented being pestered for money. Still, Poe wrote to him on November 12: "I would not trouble you so often if I was not extremely pinched. . . ."[7]

Not all of Poe's luck was bad. He sent poems he had worked on during his army days to Hatch & Dunning, a Baltimore printer. He included six new poems, and six from the 1827 volume. In December 1829, a slim new book entitled *Al Aaraaf, Tamerlane and Minor Poems* was published in an edition of two hundred fifty copies. The twenty-year-old poet eagerly awaited the reviews. The Baltimore *Minerva and Emerald* declared, "There is something in these poems so original, that we cannot help introducing them to the public as a literary curiosity, full of burning thoughts."[8] As a published poet, Poe became something of a celebrity in Baltimore. He was sometimes asked to recite his poems and sign autographs.

At last, John Allan invited Poe to visit Richmond. During the first months of 1830, Poe lived with his foster father. It is possible he simply stayed at Allan's comfortable Main Street house, writing in his bedroom. Perhaps he visited Allan's country plantation, the Byrd. During that time, he wrote five or six new poems, including a fine poem, "To Helen." It was written to honor Jane Stith Stanard, the Richmond lady he had so admired six years before.

West Point Cadet

At the end of March 1830, Poe learned that he had been accepted at the United States Military Academy. The new cadet traveled north to New York City, then up the Hudson River to West Point, arriving at the end of June. During the next two months of summer encampment, Poe lived in a tent, slept on the ground, and drilled in the heat of the sun. On September 1, the cadets began their classroom studies. Poe was quartered in Number 28 South Barracks, along with cadets Thomas W. Gibson and Timothy Pickering Jones.

At twenty-one, Poe was older than most of his fellow cadets. New cadets could be as young as sixteen. Poe's military experience and education made him seem even older than twenty-one. Cadet George Washington Cullum described Poe in a letter home: "He is thought a fellow of talent here. . . ."[9] Poe wrote

West Point cadets load a cannon during a training exercise. As a cadet at the United States Military Academy, Poe enjoyed the New York countryside and the magnificent views of the Hudson River.

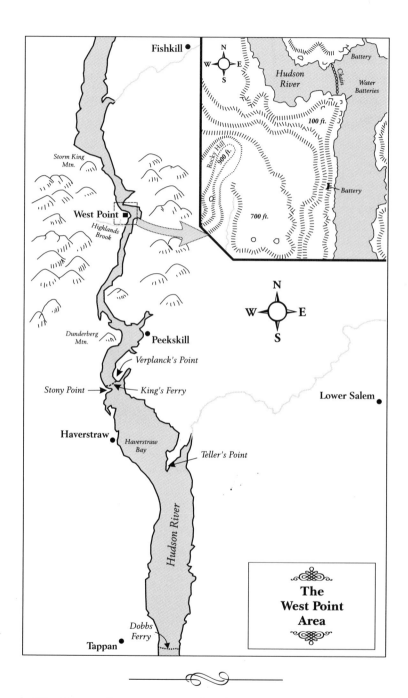

West Point, where Poe attended military school, is located in the Hudson Valley region of New York. West Point was a strategic military base during the American Revolution.

to John Allan that fall: "I have a very excellent standing in my class—in the first section in everything and have great hopes of doing well."[10]

During the previous year, widower John Allan had met a northern lady, Louisa Gabriella Patterson, and had begun courting her. Poe was shocked when he learned that Allan had remarried on October 5, 1830. He suddenly realized that Allan's second marriage ruined his hopes of an inheritance. Allan and his second wife would have children of their own. He also knew that he would have to spend five hard years at West Point before earning his commission as a lieutenant. Even then, a lieutenant's low pay would not be enough for him to live as a gentleman. As a result, Poe decided to quit his military career.

The Final Break

While living with Allan in Richmond in May 1830, Poe had received a letter from Sergeant Graves. Graves had asked for the fifty dollars Poe still owed him. In his reply letter, Poe had foolishly joked, "Mr. Allan is not very often sober—which accounts for [my being unable to get your money]."[11] Unable to get his money from Poe, in December, Graves sent that letter to Allan. The comment, "Mr. A is not very often sober" deeply insulted Allan. He wrote Poe that he never wanted to see or hear from him again.

Poe wrote to his foster father on January 3, 1831. "You sent me to W. Point like a beggar," he unhappily declared:

The same difficulties are threatening me as before at Charlottesville—and I must resign. . . . I have no more to say—except that my future life (which thank God will not endure long) must be passed in [poverty] and sickness. I have no energy left, nor health. . . . it is my intention to resign. For this end it will be necessary that you (as my . . . guardian) enclose me your written permission.[12]

Allan scribbled on the back of this letter, "I do not think the Boy has one good quality. He may do or act as he pleases . . . since I cannot believe a word he writes. His letter is the most barefaced one sided statement."[13]

Without Allan's written permission, Poe could not resign from West Point. So, Poe decided to get himself court-martialed and thrown out of the academy. Between January 7 and 27, 1831, he deliberately disobeyed orders. He failed to report for parades, roll calls, and guard duty thirteen times. He also stopped attending classes. Finally, on January 28, cadet Poe was court-martialed on charges of "Gross Neglect of Duty" and "Disobedience of Orders." The military court found him guilty, and he was dismissed from the armed services.[14]

The Struggling Poet

On February 21, 1831, Poe sent his foster father a letter from New York City, once more begging for money. "I left West Point two days ago," he wrote, "and travelling to N. York without a cloak or any other clothing of importance, I have caught a most violent cold. . . . I shall never rise from my bed—besides a

most violent cold on my lungs my ear discharges blood
. . . continually and my headache is distracting. . . ."[15]
He urged his foster father to forget the earlier insult
and send him some money.[16] Allan ignored the letter.

In New York, Poe started writing again. Before
leaving West Point, he had persuaded many of his fellow students to subscribe to a book of his poems. Most
of the cadets paid seventy-five cents each to help pay
for the publication. They mistakenly thought the book
would contain comical poems like the ones Poe had
often written at West Point. New York publisher Elam
Bliss agreed to issue five hundred copies of a new book.

In this book, Poe included carefully revised early
poems such as "Al Aaraaf" and "Tamerlane." He also
included three of his fine new poems, "To Helen,"
"Israfel," and "The City in the Sea." All three
described Poe's longing for a world of ideal beauty. In
April 1831, *Poems* by Edgar A. Poe was printed, but it
did not receive much notice. Many scholars today,
however, regard it as the best book of poems ever
written by an American poet up to that time.

In May 1831, Poe left New York. He returned to
Baltimore and moved in with his aunt Maria Clemm's
family. Neighbor Mary Devereaux remembered meeting him at that time: He was

> about five feet eight inches tall, and had dark, almost
> black hair, which he wore long. . . . His eyes were large
> and full, gray and piercing. . . . His skin was of a clear
> beautiful olive. He had a sad, melancholy look. . . .
> When he looked at you it seemed as if he could read
> your thoughts.[17]

A Story Contest

While reading the June 4, 1831, issue of the Philadelphia *Saturday Courier*, Poe learned of a short-story contest. The magazine offered a prize of one hundred dollars for the best original story submitted by December 1. Poe immediately set out to win this prize. He decided to write a collection of stories that he would call *The Tales of the Folio Club*.

Through the summer and fall, Poe worked on his stories. He endured the humble living conditions in the poor Clemm household. He also mourned the death of his twenty-four-year-old brother, Henry, on August 1, 1831, of tuberculosis.

Poe finished five stories for *The Tales of the Folio Club* in time for the contest and sent them in. In December, the prize was announced. Poe learned that the one hundred dollars had been awarded to Delia S. Bacon for a sentimental story entitled "Love's Martyr." Not only did Poe fail to win the prize, but the *Saturday Courier* had his stories. It published all five throughout the year 1832, and Poe received no money for them. If Poe had had a copyright for his writings, no one could have printed his work without his permission. Unlike today, there were no strong copyright laws in the United States then.

Bitterly disappointed, he kept on writing. In the fall of 1832, Maria Clemm moved her family to 3 Amity Street in Baltimore. Without proper clothing, Poe wore his West Point overcoat that winter. Then, in the spring of 1833, he learned that his foster father,

John Allan, had died at the age of fifty-four. When Allan's will was read, it revealed that he had left Poe nothing.

Another Writing Contest

By the spring of 1833, Poe had added six new stories to his *Tales of the Folio Club*. In June, the Baltimore *Saturday Visitor* announced another contest. It offered fifty dollars for the best story and twenty-five dollars for the best poem submitted by October 1. Full of hope, Poe sent in his latest tales as well as a new poem, "The Coliseum."

When the prizes were announced that October, the three judges declared *The Tales of the Folio Club* the best. They awarded the short-story prize to Poe's story "MS. Found in a Bottle." It was published in the *Saturday Visitor* on October 19, 1833. Poe later learned from the judges that he would have won the poetry prize, too, if he had not already won the larger fifty-dollar story prize. "MS. Found in a Bottle" is a shipwreck story. The narrator writes the strange fateful tale just before the ship he is on is sucked down by a whirlpool into a vast hole at the center of Antarctica. The manuscript telling this tale is put into a bottle and thrown overboard just before the narrator's horrible death.

Thrilled to discover he had won the prize, Poe visited each of the three judges. Businessman John H. B. Latrobe was in his office in Baltimore when Poe entered and introduced himself. "I was seated at my desk," Latrobe recalled,

. . . a gentleman entered . . . saying that he came to thank me. . . . He was dressed in black, and his frock-coat was buttoned to the throat. . . . Coat, hat, boots, and gloves had very evidently seen their best days, but so far as mending and brushing go, everything had been done . . . to make them presentable.[18]

Another of the judges was John Pendleton Kennedy. Kennedy was a well-known Baltimore lawyer and writer. Kennedy advised Poe to submit "The Visionary" from the *Folio Club* tales to the magazine *Godey's Lady's Book*. Poe received a small payment for it, and it was published in the January 1834 issue.

Thomas W. White, the editor of the *Southern Literary Messenger*, a Richmond magazine, agreed to publish Poe's story "Berenice." White also offered Poe books to review. This raised Poe's spirits and earned him a little money.

Finally, in April 1835, Kennedy wrote White a letter recommending Poe for a job on the staff at White's magazine. "He is very clever with his pen," Kennedy wrote. "And, poor fellow, he is very poor. I told him to write something for every number of your magazine, and that you might find it to your advantage to give him some permanent employ. . . ."[19]

The Clemm family needed all the help it could get. At Amity Street, Maria Clemm's son left home for good. Grandmother Poe was bedridden and required Maria Clemm's constant attention. Poe found himself spending more and more time alone with his cousin Virginia. Twelve-year-old Virginia

Baltimore lawyer and writer John Pendleton Kennedy kindly helped Poe find work.

Clemm was bright and cheerful, a beautiful girl with a pale complexion, black hair, violet eyes, and a soft voice. Poe called her Sissy, a loving form of "Sister." In time, he grew increasingly fond of her. He did not know what the future held for him. But Poe knew that being with Virginia made him more hopeful and happy.

Editor of the Southern Literary Messenger

O n July 7, 1835, Poe's grandmother died at the age of seventy-nine. The government stopped the pension she had received for her husband's army service. Poe needed money more than ever to help support his aunt and cousin. Luckily, Thomas White soon invited him to join the staff of the *Southern Literary Messenger* at a salary of ten dollars a week. Poe gratefully traveled to Richmond and took the job of assistant editor. He wrote four book reviews for the magazine's September 1835 issue and inserted three of his stories.

A Declaration of Love

During the first month he was living and working in Richmond, Poe learned some family news that upset

In this view of Richmond, Virginia, the James River can be seen to the left. It was there that Poe swam as a boy. As a young man, Poe returned to Richmond in 1835 to be a magazine editor.

him greatly. His cousin Neilson Poe was the owner of a Baltimore newspaper. As a relative concerned for her welfare, Neilson Poe had offered to take Virginia Clemm into his comfortable home. He would pay for her education and introduce her into society.

The thought of his Sissy living with Neilson was painful to Poe. He regarded Neilson as a rival for Virginia's affections. On August 29, he desperately wrote to Maria Clemm, revealing his deep feelings for his young cousin Virginia. "I am blinded with tears," he declared, while writing this letter—I have no wish to live another hour. . . . I love Virginia. . . . I cannot express in words the fervent devotion I feel towards my dear little cousin—my own darling. . . . Let me have, under her own hand, a letter, bidding me *good bye*—forever—and I may die—my heart will break—but I will say no more.[1]

The thought of losing Virginia caused Poe so much unhappiness that he drank alcohol to forget his troubles. His work at the *Southern Literary Messenger* soon suffered. When he arrived at the office on September 20, he and White argued about his drinking. Angrily, Poe quit the office. He hurried home to Baltimore.

Almost as soon as he got to Baltimore he went to the courthouse and obtained a license to marry Virginia. Maria Clemm felt thirteen-year-old Virginia was far too young to marry. She refused to allow the marriage. But she agreed at last that she and Virginia would go back with Poe to Richmond, where he would try to get his job back.

Poe sent a letter of apology to White for his behavior. In his reply, White advised his assistant to find a place to live in Richmond "where liquor is not used," and added, "No man is safe who drinks before breakfast! No man can do so, and attend to business properly."[2] He agreed to give Poe a second chance.

Poe returned to Richmond with Virginia and his aunt on October 3, 1835. They moved into a boardinghouse run by Mrs. James Yarrington, on Capitol Square, at a cost of nine dollars a week for food and lodging. While he worked for the *Southern Literary*

Messenger, Poe took charge of Virginia's education, tutoring her in some subjects himself and using his income to provide her with the best schooling he could afford.[3]

Poe at Work

With energy, Poe took on the task of improving the *Southern Literary Messenger*. He began by reprinting one of his revised *Folio Club* tales in each issue. He also wrote long book reviews and essays. In addition, his duties at the magazine included reading manuscripts, handling correspondence, and designing the layout of each issue for printing. As a reward for his hard work, by December 1835, White officially announced that Poe had become editor of the magazine.

Altogether, during 1835 and 1836, Poe reprinted in the *Southern Literary Messenger* seven of his *Tales of the Folio Club*. He also published three of his other early stories, and three new stories. In his story "The Unparalleled Adventure of One Hans Pfaall," Poe created his first science fiction tale. The story imagines a fantastic voyage to the moon by hot-air balloon. Poe had described the tale earlier to John Latrobe. "[Poe] had become so excited," Latrobe remembered,

> spoke so rapidly, [gesturing] much, that when the turn-up-side-down [of the balloon] took place, and he clapped his hands and stamped with his foot by way of emphasis, I was carried along with him, and . . . may have fancied myself the companion of his . . . journey.[4]

Many scholars and such later famed science fiction writers as Jules Verne and H. G. Wells regard "Hans Pfaall" as the first modern science fiction story ever written.

Poe's remarkable stories often included material currently being discussed in the newspapers. Readers snapped up issues of the *Southern Literary Messenger* to read about thrilling balloon flights, new scientific inventions, and exciting explorations. Poe understood the kinds of unusual subjects that would attract readers. He felt good about his skills as an editor, and felt confident about his future.[5]

Poe the Critic

Poe desired to raise the standards of American literature. He wrote more honestly about the art of writing than any other critic had ever dared before. Readers of the *Southern Literary Messenger* were amazed and amused by his essays. Poe openly attacked the writings of America's most respected authors of the day, whenever he found fault. Such famous writers as James Fenimore Cooper, Washington Irving, Ralph Waldo Emerson, William Cullen Bryant, and Henry Wadsworth Longfellow all received criticism. Longfellow, for example, was a man, Poe commented, who wrote "brilliant poems—by accident."[6]

In his book reviews, Poe praised books he liked while making fun of those he did not. "*The Swiss Heiress*," Poe declared, for example, "should be read by all who have nothing better to do."[7] His witty review of the novel *Norman Leslie* attracted attention all over the nation. The next month, he followed it with a mocking review of the novel *Paul Ulric*. "[W]hen we called *Norman Leslie* the silliest book in the world," he wrote, "we had certainly never seen *Paul Ulric*."[8]

Readers laughed with surprise and pleasure at such reviews. It was Poe's book reviews, even more than his stories and poems, that soon raised the magazine's sales from about seven hundred copies a month to about five thousand. As a reward, in February 1836, White raised Poe's pay to twelve dollars a week.

Poe believed the time had arrived when he could afford to marry Virginia. Again he pestered Maria Clemm for permission to marry her daughter. It was obvious that he and thirteen-year-old Virginia loved one another, and American society accepted marriages between cousins back then. Eventually, Maria Clemm agreed. On May 16, 1836, Poe and a friend, Thomas W. Clelland, went to the courthouse. Clelland, as witness, lied that Virginia was the legal age of twenty-one, and Poe obtained a marriage license. That evening, the Reverend Amasa Converse, a Presbyterian minister, married Poe and Virginia at Mrs. Yarrington's boardinghouse. Poe was twenty-seven years old and Virginia was only thirteen years and nine months. It was not unusual for teenagers to marry in the 1800s. But Virginia seemed especially young. Still, the newlyweds enjoyed a two-week honeymoon in Petersburg, Virginia, before returning to Richmond.

Edgar Allan Poe as a young man. At the age of twenty-seven, he married his cousin Virginia Clemm in 1836. She was only thirteen years old.

Professional Unhappiness

Poe's hard work at the *Southern Literary Messenger* made his name known in the literary world. His long hours at the office, however, kept him from working on his own writing. In frustration, he began to drink again. It was clear that Poe had a weakness for alcohol. Baltimore journalist John Hewitt recalled, "Whenever he tasted alcohol, he seldom stopped drinking it so long as he was able. . . . His taste for drink was a simple disease—no source of pleasure or excitement."[9]

Poe's drinking caused two issues of the *Southern Literary Messenger* to be delayed. Finally, in December 1836, White fired him. Poe had made the magazine nationally famous. Readership had increased so much that, in 1836, White earned a huge profit of ten thousand dollars. Yet White complained that Poe was frequently asking for money and decided to fire Poe as editor, despite his skills.[10]

Poe was not upset about being fired. He was ready for a change. Another literary magazine, the New York *Review*, was asking him for stories and essays. He also wanted very much to start a magazine of his own. He decided to go north to New York City and see if he could succeed there.

5

IN NEW YORK AND PHILADELPHIA, 1838–1841

Twenty-eight-year-old Edgar Allan Poe brought his teenage wife, Virginia, and his aunt, Maria Clemm, to New York City in February 1837. They rented an old house at 113 and a half Carmine Street. Within weeks, the economic depression of 1837 began. Poe suddenly found it very difficult to get reviewing work or to sell stories. For a while, he and his family survived by eating only bread and molasses.

The Narrative of Arthur Gordon Pym

While in Richmond, Poe had begun writing a novel, *The Narrative of Arthur Gordon Pym*. It was the story of a young man who stows away aboard a whaling ship. On the title page, Poe explained that the novel included "the details of a mutiny and [terrible] butchery

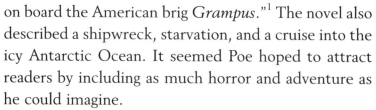

The Panic of 1837
In the spring of 1837, New York banks announced that they would no longer give gold and silver in exchange for paper money. This decision caused a national panic. Worried investors hurried to banks and withdrew their savings. Nine hundred banks without sufficient funds failed nationwide. Thousands of people lost their jobs because money suddenly became scarce. This economic depression lasted until 1843.

on board the American brig *Grampus*."[1] The novel also described a shipwreck, starvation, and a cruise into the icy Antarctic Ocean. It seemed Poe hoped to attract readers by including as much horror and adventure as he could imagine.

He completed the novel in New York and delivered it to the publisher Harper's & Co. Harper's published it in the fall of 1838. But the book seemed so unbelievable to readers that it failed to sell well.

Poe also sold two short stories, but the money did not last long. Maria Clemm rented one of their rooms to a boarder to help them survive. After a year, however, Poe admitted he could not make a living in New York. He decided to move again, this time to Philadelphia.

To Philadelphia

In Philadelphia, Poe and his family lived first at 1267 Arch Street, near the Delaware River. After that, they rented a small house on Sixteenth Street. Writer Thomas Dunn English met Poe in Philadelphia at this time. English remembered, "He was [dressed] in a plain and rather worn suit of black which was carefully brushed, and his linen was especially notable for its cleanliness. His eyes . . . were large bright and piercing, his manner easy and refined, and his tone and conversation winning."[2]

Poe sold a ghost story called "Ligeia" to a Baltimore magazine, *The American Museum*, for ten dollars. He also sold a few poems to that magazine. Then, in the winter of 1838, he agreed to assist with a textbook

Philadelphia, Pennsylvania's famed Shot Tower rises at the center of this view of the city. After failing to make a living in New York City, Poe decided to try his luck in Philadelphia.

called *The Conchologist's First Book*. Five years earlier, Thomas Wyatt had published an expensive biology book about mollusk shells. Sales were poor, and Wyatt wished to print a shorter edition at a much lower price. For a fee of fifty dollars, Poe agreed to help. "I wrote the Preface and Introduction," Poe explained, "and translated [from the original text by the French author] Cuvier, the accounts of animals etc."[3] Poe said that the new book gave "an anatomical account of each animal, together with a description of the shell which it inhabits."[4] Printed in April 1839, Wyatt successfully sold the book during lecture tours.

Burton's Gentleman's Magazine

In Philadelphia, William E. Burton, an English comic actor, was publishing a magazine called *Burton's Gentleman's Magazine*. The pages of *Burton's* were filled with sentimental short stories, theatrical gossip, and book reviews. In July 1839, Burton hired Poe as editor at a salary of ten dollars a week. Burton also promised to help Poe establish a literary magazine of his own in six months.

Poe was glad to get a steady job. He liked his rented home because Virginia was content there. She enjoyed their small garden and happily played with their coal-black kitten, which they had named Catterina.

Poe went to work at *Burton's*. In the July 1839 issue, he contributed all of the book reviews. In following issues he published his newest stories, including "The Man Who Was Used Up," "The Fall of

William E. Burton was a stage actor who also owned a magazine.
Poe went to work for Burton in July 1839 and soon began publishing
his stories in the pages of Burton's Gentleman's Magazine.

the House of Usher," and "William Wilson." "The Man Who Was Used Up" described a military man who looks handsome but turns out to be made only of a war-scarred torso and head. The rest of him consists of fake legs, arms, eyes, and other artificial body parts. "The Fall of the House of Usher" was a story that described the horrible end of a family named Usher. In the story, the Usher mansion, which is a symbol of the ruined family, crumbles and falls into a mountain lake. In "William Wilson," the narrator commits a murder. He kills a man who looks very much like him and who throughout his life has continually reminded him of his faults.

From January until June 1840, Poe published monthly installments of "The Journal of Julius Rodman." It was an adventure story about explorers in the West in 1792. Full of lengthy descriptions of geography and animal life, the writing was not very good. But Poe was desperate for money, and Burton paid him an extra three dollars a page for his stories.

It was fine stories such as "The Fall of the House of Usher" that helped establish Poe's reputation as a serious writer. The Philadelphia publishing company of Lea & Blanchard agreed to print a collection of his best stories. The two-volume book entitled *Tales of the Grotesque and Arabesque* appeared in December 1840. It included twenty-five stories, each carefully revised. The publishers printed an edition of seven hundred fifty copies, from which they took the entire profit. Poe's payment was only twenty copies of the book. The book's "grotesque" stories were mostly

Folio Club tales. The "arabesques" were Poe's tales of horror. Today, the book is regarded as one of America's best. But in 1840, it was not appreciated and did not sell well.

Poe the Codebreaker

To earn extra money, Poe began writing essays for *Alexander's Weekly Messenger*, a Philadelphia newspaper. In one issue, he attracted notice by offering to solve any secret code sent to him—in either French, Italian, Spanish, German, Latin, or Greek.[5] The magazine received as many as one hundred coded messages, and Poe solved all but one. On February 12, 1840, he complained in his column, "Do people really think that we have nothing in the world to do but to read hieroglyphics? . . . Will any body tell us how to get out of this dilemma? If we don't solve all the puzzles forwarded, their [senders] will think it is because we cannot—when we can."[6]

In time, Poe became unhappy working at *Burton's*. Burton failed to keep his promise to help Poe start a magazine of his own. When he also tried to make a cut in Poe's pay, Poe abruptly quit in May 1840.

Poe was determined to start a literary magazine he would call *Penn Magazine*. Poe wrote an advertisement to attract subscribers, contributors, and investors for the magazine. In June 1840, he distributed it as widely as he could. He sent it to fellow writers, and subscribers of *Burton's* and the *Southern Literary Messenger*. Although he attracted interest, it was not enough to start his magazine.

Graham's Magazine

In October 1840, William Burton sold his magazine to publisher George R. Graham. Graham bought Burton's list of thirty-five hundred subscribers for $3,500. He combined Burton's magazine with a magazine he owned called *The Casket*. He called the new magazine *Graham's Magazine*. Altogether it had about five thousand readers.

Poe immediately submitted to Graham a new story he had written called "The Man of the Crowd." Graham printed it in his first issue in November 1840. In "The Man of the Crowd," the narrator notices a curious old man wandering through the streets of London and decides to follow him for an entire night. As each neighborhood grows quiet, the old man moves on to another still alive with people. Finally, the narrator decides, "This old man . . . is the type and the genius of deep crime. He refuses to be alone. He is the man of the crowd."[7]

This is a reproduction of the cover of an issue of Graham's Magazine.

As a freelance writer trying to support his wife and aunt, Edgar Allan Poe worked hard to sell his poems and stories to whichever magazines and newspapers he could. Unfortunately, the little money he earned from the sales of his published works could barely keep his family fed.

6

EDITOR OF
GRAHAM'S
MAGAZINE

Poe tried a second time to start his *Penn Magazine*. He sent out another advertisement, promising that the magazine would give honest opinions on all the subjects it discussed.[1] Poe wanted to create a magazine of the highest possible quality and content. He needed five hundred subscribers to finance his magazine. But again he failed to get them. As a result, when George Graham invited him to work for *Graham's Magazine*, Poe accepted.

Magazine Editing

In February 1841, Graham hired Poe as editor. Poe would receive a salary of eight hundred dollars a year and an extra four dollars for every page of original writing he contributed. Graham, like Burton, promised that after six months he would help Poe start his own magazine.

At *Graham's Magazine*, Poe read manuscripts, wrote book reviews, and contributed a story each month. A typical issue of *Graham's* contained several short stories and poems, as well as essays on subjects of interest to readers.

Poe published an especially exciting story in the April 1841 issue. For a long time, he had had a keen interest in the world of crime. Drawing on ideas he had formed from reading books and newspapers, he constructed "The Murders in the Rue Morgue." In this story, a mother and daughter are discovered murdered in their locked room. Amateur detective C. Auguste Dupin visits the house, and by studying the clues, he solves the murders. This was an entirely new kind of story—the detective story. It was a mystery story in which the act of solving the crime was more interesting than the crime itself.

During March 1841, Poe worked on an adventure story. In *Alexander's Weekly Messenger*, he had read about a whirlpool called the Maelstrom, off the coast of Norway. He learned even more about whirlpools by reading the *Encyclopaedia Britannica*. As a result, he wrote "A Descent into the Maelstrom." It was about a fisherman who survives being sucked into the Maelstrom whirlpool by clinging to a floating wooden cask. It appeared in the May 1841 issue of *Graham's*.

A Study of Handwriting

Poe understood how to excite readers' interest in the magazine. In two issues of *Graham's* he ran articles on "Autography." In them, he examined the letters and signatures of famous Americans. The two articles showed reproductions of handwriting and autographs followed by Poe's comments. He claimed that penmanship revealed each person's character. In fact, Poe probably used the articles as a clever way to express his personal opinions about the writers' literary efforts.

Novelist James Fenimore Cooper was the author of *The Last of the Mohicans*. Poe declared, "Mr. Cooper's [handwriting] is very bad—unformed, with little of distinctive character about it. . . . the whole . . . has a constrained and school-boyish air."[2] Poet John Greenleaf Whittier's handwriting, Poe remarked, "is an ordinary clerk's hand, affording little indication of character."[3] Poe described poet Henry W. Longfellow's handwriting, however, as "remarkably good. . . . We see here plain indications of the force, vigor, and glowing richness of his literary style. . . . The man who writes thus may not accomplish much, but what he does, will always be thoroughly done."[4]

A Most Successful Magazine

Poe's original stories, sharp book reviews, and fresh ideas soon made *Graham's* the most important and surprisingly successful magazine in America. Beginning with sales of five thousand copies, *Graham's* printed twenty thousand in September 1841. That figure

American poet Henry Wadsworth Longfellow was the author of such famous poems as "The Song of Hiawatha" and "The Courtship of Miles Standish." Early in Longfellow's career, Poe cleverly criticized his writing by analyzing his handwriting.

jumped to twenty-five thousand in December 1841, and to an astonishing forty thousand in February 1842. Poe's brilliant editorship made *Graham's* the largest-selling monthly magazine in the world. Yet Graham never gave Poe a raise in salary.

Still, Poe at least had a regular paycheck. He was able to move his family to a new address at 2502 Coates Street, near Fairmount Park, in the northwest part of Philadelphia. The rooms were neat and clean, but it was a simple place. Even though Poe was poor, he liked to bring friends home to visit. He was proud of his wife, Sissy, and the aunt he had nicknamed Muddy, a loving way of saying "mother."

Maria Clemm took care of all the cleaning and cooking. Poe set aside some of his earnings and bought a harp and a piano for Virginia. On happy evenings, after dinner, Poe would play the flute, and Virginia would sing and play the harp or the piano.

A Night of Horror

The evening of January 20, 1842, was the day after Poe's thirty-third birthday. That night, while Virginia was singing and playing the piano, she suddenly broke a blood vessel in her throat. Poe stared in horror as blood poured from her mouth. He immediately ran for a doctor. It was discovered that Virginia suffered from tuberculosis, the same lung disease that had killed Poe's mother and brother, Henry.

Virginia's life seemed to be in serious danger. For two weeks, Poe nervously remained at her bedside, hoping and praying. A visitor to Poe's home remembered,

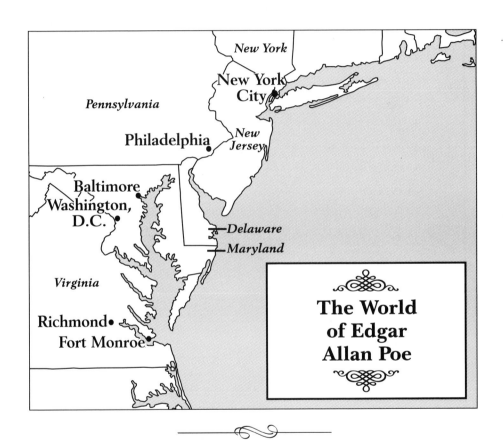

This map of the eastern region of the United States shows many of the places in which Poe lived and traveled during his career.

"no one dared to speak—Mr. Poe was so sensitive and irritable. . . ."[5]

In watching his wife suffer, Poe later declared, "I felt all the agonies of her death. . . ."[6] His fear that his beloved Virginia might die—like his mother; his foster mother, Frances Allan; and the beautiful Jane Stith Stanard—drove him nearly insane. George Graham observed, "[H]er slightest cough [caused] in him a shudder, a heart-chill, that was visible. . . . It was the hourly [fear] of her loss that made him a sad and thoughtful man. . . ."[7]

Poe hoped that country air might help Virginia recover. He moved his family to the wooded Fairmount region of Philadelphia. His worries about Virginia sometimes kept Poe from getting to work. One day in April 1842, Poe returned to the office

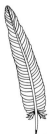

A Historic Meeting

In March 1842, a few months after Virginia fell ill, the famous English novelist Charles Dickens visited Philadelphia while on his popular American tour. Poe sent Dickens copies of his *Tales of the Grotesque and Arabesque* and requested an interview. "I shall be very glad to see you," Dickens wrote back.[8]

The next day, Poe met with Dickens at the United States Hotel on Chestnut Street. The two writers discussed American poetry, and Dickens promised to try to find a publisher for Poe's book in England. Unfortunately, he was unable to do so.

after a brief illness. He discovered a new editor sitting in his chair. Graham had hired Rufus Griswold to assist Poe with his work. But Poe, who was very sensitive, immediately assumed that Griswold was being prepared to take over his job. In a sudden rage at this imagined unfairness, Poe quit the magazine. Nothing Graham said could persuade him to return. Poe agreed to go on contributing to the magazine, but he refused to work there. In fact, free of his editorial duties, he realized he could spend more time writing stories.

7

FREELANCE WRITER

In the spring of 1842, Poe began perhaps the most creative period of his life. His stories, often so strange and frightening, reflected his own dark moods and tortured state of mind. In June, newspapers reported that the body of Mary Cecilia Rogers, a New York shopgirl, had been found floating in the Hudson River. Poe felt sure that this mystery would make a good second case for his detective C. Auguste Dupin. He quickly wrote a story called "The Mystery of Marie Roget." He claimed he had solved the murder of Mary Rogers, even though he had not. He eventually sold the story to the literary magazine *Snowden's Ladies' Companion*.

In his story "The Mystery of Marie Roget," Poe's amateur detective, C. Auguste Dupin, solved the murder of a girl whose body was found floating in a river.

Strange Tales

Poe also completed a story that he later entitled "The Oval Portrait," which he sold to *Graham's*. It was the story of a traveler who stops overnight at a country mansion. There, he is entranced by the strangely life-like portrait of a young woman. He discovers that it is a painting of the artist's wife. She had sickened and died while it was being painted, and it seemed as if her spirit had passed into the picture.

In Poe's horror story "The Masque of the Red Death," a medieval prince and a thousand friends take refuge in a walled abbey. They hope to escape a dreaded disease called the "Red Death" that is sweep-ing over the land. One night, the prince gives a masquerade ball. A mysterious guest costumed like a victim of the Red Death appears. Before the night is over, it is revealed that the frightening stranger is the Red Death itself. The prince and all his friends cannot escape. Poe finished writing this nightmare in time for the May 1842 issue of *Graham's*.

By the end of June, Poe finished "The Pit and the Pendulum." This horror story described a prisoner in Spain. In his cell, he is tortured first with the danger of falling into a deep pit. When he escapes that terror, he is next threatened by a giant blade that swings over him like a clock's pendulum. With cleverness and luck, the man does escape death.

Poe's brilliant tale "The Tell-Tale Heart" is narrated by a crazed murderer. He cannot bear to look at the blind eye of his old neighbor. "He had the eye of a vulture—a pale blue eye, with a film over it," Poe wrote.[1] The madman kills his neighbor and buries him under his floor boards. But in his guilty mind he still hears the beating of the dead man's heart. The imagined sound tortures him until he finally confesses his crime. A Boston magazine, *The Pioneer*, published this fine story, but paid only ten dollars for it.

The Dream of a Government Job

Toward the end of June 1842, Frederick W. Thomas, a lawyer and friend, wrote to Poe from Washington, D.C., informing him of a government office available that paid fifteen hundred dollars a year. Thomas urged Poe to apply for the clerkship, since it would leave him time to write.[2] Thomas himself had obtained a job as a clerk at the Treasury Department.

Poe was willing. Thomas was a good friend of President John Tyler's son Robert. He tried to use his connections to get Poe a government position in the Philadelphia Customs House. The Customs House collected taxes on imported goods. In November 1842, when the list of new customs house appointments was announced in the newspapers, Poe saw the name "Pogue." He guessed it was a misspelling of his own name, "Poe." He called on the collector, Thomas S. Smith, asking for news of his appointment to the post he wanted. Smith said no, and Poe expressed surprise, saying he knew Robert Tyler, the son of the president, had been asked to help get him the post. Smith replied, "I have received orders from *President* Tyler to make no more [appointments] and shall make none."[3] Poe left, disappointed.

A Publishing Partner

Poe still dreamed of publishing his own magazine, and in February 1843, he found a partner, Thomas C. Clarke. Clarke published a Philadelphia weekly paper called *The Saturday Museum*. Poe hoped to begin publishing his monthly magazine, which he now called *The Stylus*, in July 1843.

To give Poe and the new magazine some publicity, Clarke published a biography and portrait of Poe in the February 25, 1843, issue of *The Saturday Museum*: "[H]e is somewhat slender, about five feet, eight inches in height, and well proportioned; his complexion is rather fair; his eyes are grey and restless, exhibiting a marked nervousness. . . ."[4] Poe did not like his published portrait and declared, "I am ugly enough, God knows, but not *quite* so bad as that."[5]

Home Life

Early in the spring of 1843, the Poes moved to their fourth house in Philadelphia. It was a brick cottage constructed in the style called a half-house. It stood at 234 North Seventh Street, in the Spring Garden district of the city.

The little family furnished this house with white curtains, simple chairs, and colorful flowering plants. It was a cozy home. But in time, poverty and debts caused Poe to sell pieces of the furniture, including Virginia's piano. Still, Poe tried to be cheerful. "I rise

In the spring of 1843, Poe and his family moved into this house at 234 North Seventh Street in Philadelphia. At the end of the house, a line down the middle shows where an inside wall divided the building into two "half-houses."

early," he explained, "eat moderately, drink nothing but water. . . ."[6]

A Trip to Washington

In March 1843, Poe journeyed to Washington to try again to obtain a customs house position. He decided to approach President Tyler directly. Unfortunately, becoming nervous and excited, he allowed himself to get drunk again. In high spirits, he visited the government departments asking for contributions for *The Stylus* and enjoyed himself highly. "I believe that I am making a sensation," he drunkenly declared.[7]

Only after he got back home did he realize he had behaved badly. In embarrassment he wrote to Frederick Thomas: "Please express my regret to Mr. Fuller for making such a fool of myself. . . ."[8] President Tyler's son Robert had been shocked by Poe's condition in Washington. There was no chance now of Poe's getting a job from the president. "I blame no one but myself," Poe wrote to his friends.[9]

To make matters worse, Poe's plans for *The Stylus* collapsed completely. Disturbed by Poe's drinking and in serious difficulties with his own magazine, Thomas Clarke withdrew his support.

"The Gold Bug" and "The Black Cat"

Poe sat at his writing table, always alert. Every time he heard Virginia cough, it caused him a pang of worry. In his struggle to earn money, he continued writing sensational, original stories. His story "The Gold Bug," for instance, became a great success. It was the story of a search for buried pirate treasure on Sullivan's Island, South Carolina. Poe included information he remembered from his time in South Carolina when, as a young soldier, he had explored Sullivan's Island with the biologist Dr. Edmund Ravenel. *Graham's Magazine* was eager to buy the story at a cheap price. But Poe learned that the *Dollar Newspaper* was offering a prize of a hundred dollars in a story contest. He entered "The Gold Bug," and it won the prize. The story appeared in the paper in June 1843. It proved so popular that it was soon reprinted in the *Dollar Newspaper* for readers who had missed it the first time and also in the *Saturday Courier*. In addition, playwright Silas S. Steele rewrote the story as a play. An audience applauded the performance on August 8, 1843, at Philadelphia's Walnut Street Theatre.

Another story, "The Black Cat," was published in the August 19, 1843, issue of the *United States Saturday Post*. Again Poe drew on his own personal fears to create a tale of horror and suspense. Poe knew he sometimes went into a rage when he was drinking. "The Black Cat" described how a drunkard could harm those he loved.

The narrator of the story kills a pet black cat while in a drunken fury. Later, the appearance of a second black cat into the household fills the narrator with guilty feelings. In another drunken rage, he kills his wife. He hides her corpse behind a wall in the cellar of their house. The police investigate but find nothing, until the killer casually taps the wall. The police hear the howling of the black cat. The narrator had accidentally

From "The Black Cat"

"One night, returning home much intoxicated, from one of my haunts about town, I fancied that the cat avoided my presence. I seized him; when in his fright at my violence, he inflicted a slight wound upon my hand with his teeth. The fury of a demon instantly possessed me."[10]

walled the cat up with the corpse. Poe sold this gory tale to *Godey's Lady's Book*.

Poe as a Lecturer

Through the fall of 1843, Poe worked steadily on new stories. Yet he remained in constant need of money. To raise some cash, he decided to try lecturing. In those days, before movies, radio, or television, people often enjoyed the entertainment of paying to listen to a lecture. On November 21, 1843, Poe gave his first talk in Philadelphia on the subject "Poetry in America." His reputation as a critic and the recent popularity of "The Gold Bug" drew a large audience interested in what he had to say.

Poe spoke with intelligence in a voice that was soft and rich. He read several poems with the dramatic power of an actor, paying special attention to the rhythm. Audiences were enthusiastic about his performance.[11] Poe earned about one hundred dollars, a very welcome sum of money.

In the fall of 1843, Poe became a public speaker. His lectures were quite popular for a time. To improve his appearance, he shaved off his side whiskers and grew a moustache.

He repeated the lecture in Wilmington, Delaware, a week later, and on January 31, 1844, he spoke at the Odd Fellows Hall in Baltimore. He charged twenty-five cents for tickets. During the spring of 1844, he gave his talk in Reading, Pennsylvania, and elsewhere. To improve his appearance, he even shaved off his side whiskers and grew a moustache. By the summer, however, it grew too hot to attract people indoors to lectures. Poe returned home to his writing.

Additional Stories

More fantastic stories flowed from Poe's pen. "The Oblong Box" described an artist transporting his wife's coffin by sea. When the ship suddenly sinks, the artist refuses to save himself. Instead, he goes down with the oblong box containing the corpse, rather than abandon it.

In "The Premature Burial," Poe described a cataleptic, a man subject to fits of unconsciousness. While lying in a ship's narrow bunk, the man in a terrible dream believes he has been buried alive.

Poe also wrote another detective story called "The Purloined Letter." When an important diplomatic letter is stolen, the amateur detective C. Auguste Dupin is again called on for help. Using his excellent mental skills, Dupin discovers the letter in the home of the suspected thief.

Back in New York City

Even though troubled by poverty and Virginia's illness, Poe had achieved a lot during his six years in

Philadelphia. He had proven himself a skilled magazine editor and had published thirty-one stories, including several masterpieces. In the spring of 1844, however, he thought he might earn more money in New York. On April 6, Poe and Virginia started out for New York City. After closing up the Spring Garden house, Maria Clemm would follow them in a few weeks.

By train, Poe and Virginia traveled across New Jersey to the city of Perth Amboy. From there, a steamboat carried them into the bay of the Hudson River. On the afternoon of April 7, they docked in New York City. Poe wrote to his aunt: "I feel in excellent spirits & have'nt [drunk] a drop. . . ."[12]

"The Balloon Hoax"

Poe had a clever idea he thought would raise quick cash. He wrote a story in such a way that readers would think the events had really happened. In his story, Poe described a hot-air balloon voyage from England that ended at Fort Moultrie, South Carolina. Within a week of his arrival in New York, he sold the tall tale to the New York *Sun*.

On April 13, 1844, the newspaper announced in large headlines:

ASTOUNDING NEWS!
BY EXPRESS VIA NORFOLK!
THE ATLANTIC CROSSED IN THREE DAYS!
Signal triumph of Mr. Monck Mason's FLYING
MACHINE!!!![13]

Poe's "The Balloon Hoax" brought crowds swarming to the offices of the *Sun*. Poe happily recalled the excitement of people as they scrambled to buy copies of the newspaper.[14]

Country Living

Poe earned only a few dollars for "The Balloon Hoax." He soon discovered that life in New York was as hard as it had been in Philadelphia.

In the sunny spring weather, Poe sometimes went out for a stroll. One day, he wandered up the Bloomingdale Road to what is now about Eighty-fourth Street and Broadway. He stopped at the country farmhouse of Patrick Brennan. The Brennan farm was a lovely, quiet place, and the Brennans seemed to be friendly people. Virginia had begun suffering coughing attacks more often, and the idea of a country home attracted Poe. He asked the Brennans if he could rent rooms with them. They agreed, and in the early summer of 1844, the Poes moved in.

Poe enjoyed the calm country life. He wrote to a friend: "I scribble all day, and read all night. . . ."[15]

Whenever Poe finished writing a story or article, Maria Clemm would carry it into the city. She visited newspapers and magazines, trying to sell each of them. The income provided the family with just enough to live on. In September 1844, she called on editor N. P. Willis at the New York *Mirror*, trying to sell some of Poe's work. She persuaded Willis to hire Poe as a regular newspaper contributor. At first Poe worked at home, but he impressed Willis whenever he visited the *Mirror* office. Eventually, Willis invited him to join the newspaper staff.

During the few months he worked at the newspaper, Poe's behavior was perfect. He was never late, never drunk, and he always worked hard.

The Poes moved back into the city. They lived first in a cramped apartment at 85 Amity Street. Then they moved into a boardinghouse on 195 East Broadway. It was while working at the *Mirror* that Poe published the poem that would make him nationally famous.

$\boxed{8}$

THE RAVEN

Once upon a midnight dreary, while I pondered, weak and weary,
Over many a quaint and curious volume of forgotten lore,
While I nodded, nearly napping, suddenly there came a tapping,
As of some one gently rapping, rapping at my chamber door.
"'Tis some visitor," I muttered, "tapping at my chamber door—Only this and nothing more."

—From Poe's "The Raven"[1]

During the winter of 1844 and into the new year of 1845, Poe wrote a poem that would change his life. He carefully plotted out the verses. Beginning with "Once upon a midnight dreary," he described a man whose late-night studies are interrupted by a strange

In this illustration for Poe's poem "The Raven," a man is terrorized by a bird that perches above his door. The haunting rhythms of "The Raven" made Poe a famous poet.

visitor. It is a lost pet bird, a raven, who has learned to speak the single word "Nevermore." The bird finds a perch above the door. The man is mourning the death of his loved one, Lenore. Yet every time he asks the raven a hopeful question about her, the bird blackly croaks, "Nevermore." In despair, the man finally shouts for the bird to "Take thy beak from out my heart, and take thy form from off my door!" The raven only responds, "Nevermore." In "The Raven," Poe had constructed a poem with a hypnotic rhythm that was unforgettable.

Poe's Masterpiece

Poe realized he had written a masterpiece. One day, he met fellow poet William Ross Wallace on a New York City street, and informed him that he had just written the best poem ever.

Poe then read the verses in his rich, impressive voice. When he was done, Wallace declared, "Poe—they are fine; uncommonly fine."

"Fine!" exclaimed Poe, "I tell you it's the greatest poem that was ever written."[2]

Poe quickly sold "The Raven" to the *American Whig Review* for its February issue. He also excitedly had it printed in advance in the New York *Evening Mirror* newspaper on January 29, 1845. It is believed he was paid no more than ten dollars for the poem.

"The Raven" was a huge, immediate success. No American poem had ever been more popular. Poe became famous throughout the United States almost overnight. His name became known even as far away as England. English poet Elizabeth Barrett wrote to him: "This vivid writing—this *power which is felt*—has produced a sensation here in England. Some of my friends are taken by the fear of it and some by the music. I hear of persons who are haunted by the 'Nevermore.'"[3] Before long, Poe became so closely identified with this one poem that he received the nickname "The Raven."

At the *Broadway Journal*

Poe left the *Mirror* and joined another newspaper. On February 21, 1845, he made arrangements to become a partner at *The Broadway Journal* with John Bisco and Charles F. Briggs. In addition to editorial duties, Poe promised to supply some original writing each week. As a partner for the first time, he would be paid one third of the newspaper's profits.

To attract readers to *The Broadway Journal*, Poe continued a literary feud he had begun while at the *Mirror*. Poe had once admired poet Henry W. Longfellow greatly. But he believed Longfellow's poem "Midnight Mass for the Dying Year" was similar in many ways to Alfred Lord Tennyson's poem "The Death of the Old Year." Poe publicly accused Longfellow of stealing ideas from Tennyson. Some readers agreed with Poe. Others angrily defended Longfellow.

An article in the March 8 *Weekly Mirror* suggested that Poe could have stolen "The Raven" from an anonymous poem called "The Bird of the Dream." Poe quickly defended himself in print in *The Broadway*

Journal. The "Little Longfellow War" went on for weeks, attracting readers.

Personal Problems

On February 28, 1845, Poe successfully gave a lecture on American poetry to an audience of about three hundred in New York. When he attempted to repeat his talk in March, however, a freezing rainstorm kept people from attending. His job at *The Broadway Journal* was stressful. In addition, his newspaper income never reached the level he had hoped. Poe complained bitterly about the long hours he worked.[4]

Feeling deeply depressed, Poe began drinking again. At the end of May 1845, poet James Russell Lowell visited Poe and reported, "I have the impression he was a little soggy with drink—not tipsy—but as if he had been holding his head under a pump to cool it."[5]

In time, Briggs decided to quit the newspaper partnership. On July 14, Poe made a new contract with Bisco alone. They agreed to share the profits fifty-fifty. To fill out the pages in the paper, Poe sometimes reused old stories and poems, signing them "Littleton Barry," so his own name would not appear too often.

Much of the stress in Poe's life was caused by his worry about his sick wife. Writer Thomas H. Chivers saw Poe one day in the summer of 1845 staggering down Nassau Street, drunk. Chivers brought Poe home to bed, and Maria Clemm sadly exclaimed, "Oh! I do believe that the poor boy is deranged! His wife is now at the point of death. . . ."[6]

A New Book and a Failed Newspaper

In July 1845, the New York publishing house of Wiley & Putnam published twelve stories under the title *Tales* by Edgar A. Poe. Poe received a royalty of eight cents per copy on books that sold for fifty cents. He had revised each story carefully. He was always trying to improve his writing. The slight success of Poe's *Tales* encouraged Wiley & Putnam to agree to print a volume of Poe's poems also. *The Raven and Other Poems* was published in September. In the preface,

Virginia's Valentine's Poem

On Valentine's Day, 1846, Virginia Poe wrote her husband a Valentine poem in which the first letter of each line spelled his name:

Ever with thee I wish to roam—
Dearest my life is thine.
Give me a cottage for my home
And a rich old cypress vine,
Removed from the world with its sin and care
And the tattling of many tongues.
Love alone shall guide us when we are there—
Love shall heal my weakened lungs;
And Oh the tranquil hours we'll spend,
Never wishing that others may see!
Perfect ease we'll enjoy, without thinking to lend
Ourselves to the world and its glee—
Ever peaceful and blissful we'll be.[7]

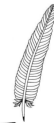

Poe declared, "With me poetry has been not a purpose, but a passion."[8]

Poe's struggles failed to make *The Broadway Journal* profitable. On October 24, 1845, Bisco sold his share of the newspaper to Poe for fifty dollars. Poe had to borrow the money. On December 26, when the loan was due, he could not repay it. As a result, *The Broadway Journal* went out of business.

A Literary War

Poe needed a change in his life. In the late spring of 1846, he moved his family to Fordham, New York, about thirteen miles north of New York City. He rented a simple cottage for one hundred dollars a year. It was a charming, quiet place surrounded by cherry trees and lilac bushes. On the ground floor inside was a sitting room, a small back room, and a kitchen. There were two more cramped but clean rooms in the attic.

Poe decided to write a series of articles, profiles of New York City authors. From May, the month he moved to Fordham, until October 1846, he published his articles in *Godey's Lady's Book*, a very popular magazine. The articles sharply attacked more than one well-known New York writer.

His profile of writer Thomas Dunn English caused a heated controversy. Among other things, Poe claimed that English was uneducated.[9] When English read the article, he went into a rage. On June 23, "Mr. English's Reply to Mr. Poe" appeared in the *Mirror*. In it, English made a hateful personal attack on Poe. As a result, Poe sued English in court for slander. Months later, a judge ordered the *Mirror* to pay Poe $492 in damages and costs. English snuck out of the city, fearing he would be arrested.

During this literary feud, South Carolina novelist William Gilmore Simms advised Poe to try to control his temper, which was hurting his reputation.[10] But Poe ignored this advice. His critical articles in 1846 lost him many friends and made him many enemies.

In November 1846, while in the midst of his bitter quarrel with English, Poe published in *Godey's Lady's Book* another fine tale, "The Cask of Amontillado." It was a story of revenge. It described a wine lover who is lured to the wine cellar of his enemy. There, he is chained and left to die, sealed behind a new wall of brick and mortar.

Life in Fordham

Family friend Mary Gove often visited Fordham in the fall of 1846. She later wrote her impressions of the Poe family. She described Maria Clemm as a tall, strong, dignified lady. Even though she was twenty-four, Virginia Poe looked very young, Gove recalled: "Her pale face, her brilliant eyes, and her raven hair gave her an unearthly look. . . ."[11]

Unable to help his wife, Poe suffered feelings of dark guilt. He was tired and ill, and Virginia's health seemed to worsen every day. For many weeks, he nursed Virginia and nearly stopped writing altogether. He did begin one new poem, however. It was called "Ulalume." It would be published in December 1847 in the *American Review*. It described a mournful man who wanders to the burial place of his dead wife.

"Then I Can Die in Peace"

Virginia's wasting disease progressed. The tuberculosis bacteria slowly destroyed her lungs. Each day, she found it harder to breathe. Her condition made Poe sick with worry. Writer friends tried to help the Poes. On December 15, 1846, the New York *Morning Express* announced that both Poe and his wife were very ill, and asked the public to come to their aid.[12]

One New York widow, Marie Louise Shew, responded by raising sixty dollars in donations, as well as a feather bed and sheets and blankets for Virginia's comfort. Poe, although a proud man, wrote humble thanks to those who sent assistance.

Virginia realized she could not live much longer. She asked her mother to look after Poe when she was gone. On January 30, 1847, Virginia Poe's long suffering ended. She died at the age of twenty-four.

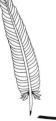

From "Ulalume"

And I cried—"It was surely October,
On this very night of the year,
That I journeyed—I journeyed down here!—
That I brought a dread burden down here—
On this night, of all nights in the year,
Ah, what demon has tempted me here?"[13]

Unbearable Grief

On the day of Virginia's funeral, her body was wrapped in fine linen supplied by Marie Louise Shew. In life, Virginia had never been photographed or had her picture drawn. So, before her burial, a family friend painted a watercolor sketch of her as she lay in her coffin.

Wearing his army overcoat, Poe followed the solemn funeral procession to a burial vault in the graveyard of the Fordham Dutch Reformed Church. He was in a state of total shock. He could not bear the thought of life without Virginia. Maria Clemm and Marie Louise Shew had to watch over him. One or the

The Poe cottage in Fordham, New York, was where Poe's beloved wife, Virginia, died in 1847. It was also the last place Poe would ever call home.

After his wife's death, Poe greatly depended on his aunt Maria Clemm (seen here), whom he lovingly called "Muddy."

other of them often sat at his bedside each night until he fell asleep. He could not stand to be alone.

In the months following Virginia's death, Poe seemed close to insanity. "[T]he loss of his wife was a sad blow to him," one friend exclaimed. "[S]he was his all."[14] Another friend remembered, "Many times, after the death of his beloved wife, was he found . . . sitting beside her tomb almost frozen in the snow, where he had wandered from his bed weeping and wailing."[15]

LAST DAYS OF THE RAVEN

Two dreams drove Edgar Allan Poe onward during his final years. One was the dream of finding another woman who would love and care for him. The other was his dream of publishing his own literary magazine. "It is the grand purpose of my life," he declared, "from which I have never swerved."[1] But both dreams would prove difficult to obtain.

Marie Louise Shew

Kindly Marie Louise Shew had nursed both Virginia and Poe. After Virginia's death, she became the object of Poe's affections. He wrote her romantic poems and letters, and for a time, they were close friends.

One Sunday afternoon in May 1847, Poe visited her at her house on West Tenth Street in New York

City. Outside, church bells were constantly ringing at nearby Grace Church. Shew remembered Poe's saying he wanted to write a poem, but could find no inspiration. She offered to help. As they sat together, Poe complained about the noise of the bells at Grace Church. Shew took this complaint as a cue and wrote on a piece of paper, "The Bells," then began to write a poem that imitated his style. Poe then penned seven lines of his own, describing the sound of silver wedding bells. Then Shew suggested iron bells, and Poe wrote, describing them. Much later, he revised the poem, adding descriptions of golden and brass bells. It was a poem with tremendous rhythmic effect. He sent it to *Sartain's Union*, a Philadelphia magazine, where it was published.

Shew felt sorry for Poe and liked him very much. But she did not want to marry him. Finally, she was forced to end their friendship. Sadly, he accepted the rejection, writing to her, "Unless some true and tender and pure womanly love saves me, I shall hardly last a year longer, alone!"[2]

Eureka

For months, Poe had been working on a long essay entitled *Eureka*. "He never liked to be alone," Maria Clemm remembered. "I always sat with him when he was writing, and gave him a cup of hot coffee every hour or two."[3]

In *Eureka*, Poe described his concept of the universe and man's relationship with God. It was a difficult work to understand, full of fantastic ideas.

"To the few who love me and whom I love—to those who feel rather than to those who think—to the dreamers and those who put faith in dreams as in the only realities—I offer this Book of Truths," he wrote in his dedication.[4]

Poe gave a public reading of the essay at the New-York Historical Society on February 3, 1848. It was a stormy evening, however, and only about sixty people attended. One person who attended called Poe's lecture "the most intense brilliancy."[5] Another listener, however, found the lecture confusing and boring. He declared, "It drove people from the room. . . ."[6]

Annie Richmond

Poe gave another lecture in Lowell, Massachusetts, on July 10, 1848. His subject was "The Poets and Poetry of America." Listeners filled the seats at Wentworth Hall. This lecture was a great success, and it was in Lowell that Poe met Nancy Richmond. He playfully called her Annie. Annie Richmond was a happily married woman with a young daughter. But that did not stop Poe from instantly falling in love with her.

Before the end of July, Poe decided to return to his hometown, Richmond, Virginia. He still dreamed of finding subscribers for his literary magazine, *The Stylus*. In Richmond, he spent his time instead getting drunk. Poe visited the MacKenzie family and saw his sister, Rosalie. He also drunkenly challenged the editor of the *Richmond Examiner* to a duel that did not take place. His friends tried to get him sober, but finally decided instead to send him home to New

York. He failed to get a single new subscriber for *The Stylus*.

Sarah Helen Whitman

Soon after falling in love with Annie Richmond, Poe also began to court a woman named Sarah Helen Whitman. She was a forty-five-year-old widow, six years older than Poe. She lived in Providence, Rhode Island, with her mother and her sister. Whitman was a poet, and in the summer of 1848, she began exchanging poems and letters with Poe.

Poe journeyed to Providence in September in order to visit her. During his four-day stay, he called on her every day. He even dared to put his arm around her waist as they sat together in a cemetery.

Whitman was not sure that she could love him. She had heard of Poe's reputation as a drinker and as a man who started quarrels. In letters, she asked him what he had to say about his bad reputation. Poe replied, saying he could not believe people could have bad impressions of him, and expressing his distress that such opinions were common.[7]

In Mad Despair

Poe desperately wanted to be loved. He wanted Sarah Helen Whitman, but he wanted Annie Richmond even more. In early November 1848, he returned to Lowell, Massachusetts. He pleaded with Richmond to leave her husband and run away with him. Gently but firmly, she refused. Although she felt real affection for Poe, she could never abandon her husband and daughter.

Poe returned to his hotel feeling miserable. The next morning, November 5, he bought two ounces of laudanum and took a train to Boston. Laudanum was a common medicine in the 1800s, a painkiller containing the powerful drug opium. In Boston, Poe wrote a letter to Annie, reminding her that she had promised to be with him when he lay on his deathbed.[8] He then told her where to find him in Boston and said he planned to commit suicide. Putting the letter in an envelope, he swallowed an ounce of the laudanum and set out for the post office. Poe did not realize that the stomach cannot tolerate an opium overdose. On the sidewalk, he suddenly began vomiting. His suicide attempt failed to kill him. It only made him very sick.

As soon as he was able, Poe traveled to Providence to ask Sarah Helen Whitman to marry him. He was drunk and sick when he entered her home on November 9. Whitman later remembered how Poe arrived at her house terrified and excited, begging her to save him from some awful fate. Her mother whispered that she should promise him anything he wanted, in order to calm him.

Sarah Helen Whitman had sincere feelings for Poe. She agreed to marry him. She insisted, however, that at any sign of his drinking she would cancel the wedding. On November 14, Poe took the steamboat for New York. On his return to Fordham, he wrote Annie Richmond, telling her all that had happened. He declared, "I CANNOT live, unless I can feel your sweet, gentle, loving hand pressed upon my forhead. . . ."[9]

Torn between Annie Richmond and Sarah Helen Whitman, Poe seemed very nearly insane.

A Return to Providence

Sarah Helen Whitman arranged for Poe to give another lecture in Providence. On the evening of December 20, 1848, Poe lectured to an audience of eighteen hundred people at the Franklin Lyceum. His subject was "The Poetic Principle." In his talk, Poe insisted that a poem needed to be short enough to be read in a half hour. After half an hour, he insisted, readers lose interest. The effect of the poem is lost. He defined poetry as *The Rhythmical Creation of Beauty*.[10] To illustrate his beliefs, he read aloud poems by such poets as Percy Bysshe Shelley, Henry W. Longfellow, William Cullen Bryant, George Gordon Lord Byron, and Alfred Lord Tennyson.

During the lecture, Sarah Helen Whitman sat in the front row. She was proud of Poe's great success. Her mother, however, thought Poe was a fortune hunter. She instructed her lawyer to draw up a legal document. It would ensure that Poe could never control her daughter's money and property if they married. Two days after his Providence lecture, Poe signed the document, although it injured his pride to do so. That night, Poe got drunk. Whitman's mother was outraged, and Poe had to swear again that he would never take another drink.

Poe wrote to Maria Clemm on December 23, explaining that he and Whitman would be married on Christmas. But that same day, Whitman received an anonymous letter. It stated that Poe had been seen drinking a glass of wine that very morning. Resentfully, Whitman told Poe there would be no wedding. Poe stormed away from the house, saying she and her family had insulted him. Although she received a letter from him in which he vowed to stay away from "literary" women like her, Whitman never saw him again.[11]

Final Writings

Although shaken in spirit, Poe continued to write. In 1849, he published two stories, "Hop Frog" and "Landor's Cottage," in a popular Boston magazine, *The Flag of Our Union*. He also wrote a hoax story entitled "Von Kempelen and His Discovery." It was about a man who was thought to have discovered a process for making gold. The feel of his pen scratching across sheets of his favorite blue paper eased Poe's nervous tension.

Poe realized by now that Annie Richmond could not be his. But he honored her with a special poem, "For Annie." He also wrote a poem to show his love for his dear aunt, Maria Clemm, entitled "To My Mother."

When a few magazines having business difficulties suddenly canceled payment for some of his writings, Poe fell into a deep depression. In late April, forty-year-old Poe wrote: "[M]y sadness is unaccountable, and this makes me the more sad. I am full of dark forebodings. Nothing cheers or comforts me. My life seems wasted. . . ."[12] Poe wrote one more poem during this disappointing time. He called it "Annabel

Lee." Once again he used his favorite theme, the grief a man feels at the death of a beautiful woman.

The Stylus

In April 1849, Poe received a letter that suddenly made him feel more hopeful. Edward H. N. Patterson was a young admirer of Poe who lived in Oquawka, Illinois. He sent Poe a serious business proposal. Patterson wanted to publish a literary magazine with Poe as its editor.

If they could get a thousand subscribers in advance, Patterson would back the magazine, while Poe would be in charge of the editorial work.[13] Patterson would pay for all the printing and mailing costs, and they would split the profits equally. To obtain the thousand subscribers, Poe decided to make a lecture tour in the South and West. He would begin in Richmond.

A Fateful Journey

On June 29, 1849, Poe set off southward from Brooklyn, New York, by steam ferry. He kissed Maria

From "Annabel Lee"

It was many and many a year ago,
In a kingdom by the sea,
That a maiden there lived whom you may know
By the name of Annabel Lee;
And this maiden she lived with no other thought
Than to love and be loved by me.[14]

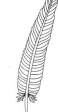

Clemm good-bye. "God bless you, my own darling mother," he told her, "Do not fear for Eddy! See how good I will be while I am away from you, and will come back to love and comfort you."[15]

In Philadelphia, he began to drink heavily. He got sick and began to think he was being followed by murderers. He may even have been arrested for drunkenness. The entire visit became a confused nightmare in his mind.

A week after his arrival in Philadelphia, he wrote to Maria Clemm:

This is an illustration Poe used to help advertise The Stylus, *the magazine he dreamed of establishing. A stylus is an ancient writing tool used to make marks on clay tablets.*

My dear, dear Mother,— I have been so ill—have had the cholera, or spasms quite as bad, and can now hardly hold the pen. . . .

The very instant you get this, come to me. The joy of seeing you will almost [make up] for our sorrows. We can but die together. It is no use to reason with me now; I must die. . . . For your sake it would be sweet to live, but we must die together. You have been all to me, darling, ever beloved mother, and dearest, truest friend.[16]

Poe stayed a day or two with publisher John Sartain. As he sobered, he slowly seemed to recover his wits. Philadelphia friends took up a collection so Poe could continue on his journey. They saw him off on the train to Baltimore on July 13. From Baltimore, Poe traveled by steamboat to Richmond. When he arrived on July 14, he took a room at the Swan Tavern and went to bed. He still felt miserable and sick.

In another letter to Maria Clemm, he declared, "Oh God, my Mother, shall we ever again meet? If possible, oh, COME! My clothes are so horrible and I am so ill."[17] But she had no money for traveling.

Another Lecture

Poe gave his lecture on "The Poetic Principle" in Richmond on August 17, 1849. Only about one hundred people paid the twenty-five-cent ticket price. They listened almost hypnotized when Poe recited "The Raven."

The *Richmond Examiner* described Poe as "a man of very decided genius. Indeed we know of no other writer in the United States who has half the chance to be remembered in literary history."[18]

Elmira Royster Shelton

On a Sunday morning in August, Poe knocked at the door at 2407 East Grace Street. It was the Richmond home of Sarah Elmira Royster Shelton. She was the same woman he had loved so many years before, when they were both teenagers. Now she was a widow.

Elmira later recalled that Poe arrived just as she was preparing to leave for church. She recognized him immediately, but, flustered by their sudden meeting, she excused herself and went to church. However, she invited him to call on her again.

During his next visit, Poe declared that he still loved her and wanted to marry her. "I laughed at it," she remembered, "[but] he looked very serious and said he was in earnest and had been thinking about it for a long time. . . . I told him that . . . he must give me time to consider of it."[19]

During their visits together, the two discovered the truth of what had happened twenty-two years before. To stop their romance, her father had sent her off to relatives and had intercepted Poe's letters. He had guessed that Poe would never inherit any of John Allan's money. Before long, Elmira became charmed by Poe's attention. In September, Poe wrote to Maria Clemm: "I think she loves me more devotedly than any one I ever knew & I cannot help loving her in return."[20]

Meanwhile, Poe continued to visit other old Richmond friends. He was often invited to homes to recite his poetry. On September 14, he traveled to Norfolk, Virginia, to give his lecture. He also gave it again in Richmond on September 24.

The Final Journey

Plans for his wedding with Elmira Royster Shelton were now set. A date was chosen, October 17. Poe decided to go back to New York to prepare for his move to Richmond. He expected to return in two weeks, bringing Maria Clemm with him.

Poe stopped to see Elmira on September 26. She recalled that he seemed sad and ill. She checked his pulse, and worried that he was too sick to begin his journey. The next day, she learned that he had sailed for Baltimore, despite his illness.[21]

Poe was aboard the Baltimore boat that left on September 27. His next five days remain a mystery. It is almost certain he got drunk. On October 3, 1847, Joseph Walker, a worker at the Baltimore *Sun*, found Poe lying in the gutter of Lombard Street. Poe was barely conscious, and Walker immediately sent for Dr. J. E. Snodgrass. Poe was taken to Washington College Hospital. For several days, he tossed and turned in feverish pain. Dr. John J. Moran did all he could for the stricken writer. Sadly, though, forty-year-old Edgar Allan Poe died on Sunday morning, October 7, 1849.

It is uncertain exactly what caused Poe's death. His alcoholism may have contributed. Some have theorized that he may have had diabetes or a brain tumor. It has also been suggested he may have been bitten by a diseased animal and died of rabies.

On October 8, a dark, rainy day, a black-plumed hearse carried Poe's coffin to the Presbyterian Cemetery at Fayette and Green streets in Baltimore. He was buried in the Poe family plot. The service was conducted by a distant relative, the Reverend William T. D. Clemm. In 1875, Poe would be reburied in another part of the cemetery. Today, Virginia Poe and Maria Clemm are both buried by his side.

Private and Public Mourning

Edgar Allan Poe's death affected those who loved and admired him. His cousin Neilson Poe wrote to Maria Clemm: "Edgar has seen so much of sorrow—had so little reason to be satisfied with life—that, to him, the change can scarcely be said to be a misfortune."[22]

In another letter to Maria Clemm, Elmira Royster Shelton grieved, "I cannot begin to tell you what my feelings were as the horrible truth forced itself upon me! . . . My heart is overwhelmed—yes, ready to burst! Oh, my dear Edgar, shall I never behold your dear face & hear your sweet voice . . ."[23]

The Baltimore *Sun* newspaper publicly commented,

> We regret to learn that Edgar A. Poe, Esq., the distinguished American poet, scholar and critic, died in this city yesterday morning, after an illness of four or five days. This announcement, coming so sudden and unexpected, will cause [deep] regret among all who admire genius, and have sympathy for the [weaknesses] too often attending it.[24]

Poe's Gift to Literature

Poe was considered an unhappy failure by many in his lifetime. But he left behind a body of writing as great as any in American literature. Altogether, he wrote thirty-one poems, sixty-seven stories, and one novel, as well as countless book reviews, essays, and articles.

Poe's critical writings are greatly admired by many modern critics. Famed critic Edmund Wilson wrote: "[Poe's] literary articles and lectures [are] surely . . . the most remarkable body of criticism ever produced in the United States. . . . [For genius] he stands on higher ground than any other American writer of his time."[25]

Poe's early poems were most often poems of sad romance, while his later poems often concerned death and yearning. Today, his later poems are his most famous. The careful rhymes and heavy rhythms in such poems as "Ulalume," "The Bells," and "The Raven" are unforgettable. Their effects reveal Poe's sensitive nature, his passion, and his pain.

As a short-story writer, Poe was truly original and amazing. He wrote the first modern science fiction story and the first modern detective stories. It is probably Poe's horror stories, however, that have left the greatest mark. Such stories as "The Fall of the House of Usher," "The Masque of the Red Death," "The Pit and the Pendulum," "The Tell-Tale Heart," "The Cask of Amontillado," and "The Black Cat" still thrill readers today with a real sense of terror. These stories of death, murder, torture, and insanity reflect Poe's own personal fears.

Edgar Allan Poe is remembered today as much for his tragic life as for his haunting poems and stories.

It is easy to imagine Edgar Allan Poe's feelings as he toiled through his difficult life. One only needs to read his essays, poems, and stories. "I am full of dark forebodings," he once admitted in a letter. "Nothing cheers or comforts me. My life seems wasted—the future looks a dreary blank. . . ." But he added, "I will struggle on and 'hope against hope.'"[26]

CHRONOLOGY

1809—Born in Boston, Massachusetts, on January 19.

1810—Father, David Poe, deserts his pregnant wife and two children.

1811—Mother, Eliza Poe, dies in Richmond, Virginia, on December 8; Edgar Poe is taken into the home of Frances and John Allan; As they raise him, he becomes known as Edgar Allan Poe.

1815—Travels to London, England, where Allan establishes a branch office.

1818—Attends a boarding school at Stoke Newington, **–1820** England; Returns to Richmond with the Allans in August 1820.

1820—Attends local Richmond schools. **–1824**

1825—Falls in love with Sarah Elmira Royster.

1826—Enters the University of Virginia in February; Runs up large debts and is withdrawn by John Allan in December.

1827—After arguing with John Allan, travels to Boston; Enlists as a private in the United States Army; Publishes *Tamerlane and Other Poems*; Travels with his artillery regiment to Fort Moultrie.

1828—Travels with regiment to Fort Monroe, Virginia.

1829—Promoted to the rank of sergeant major; Learns of his foster mother's death, February 28; Hires a substitute and is released from the army; Visits Poe relatives in Baltimore, Maryland, including Aunt Maria Clemm and cousin Virginia Clemm; Publishes *Al Aaraaf, Tamerlane and Minor Poems*.

1830—Enters the United States Military Academy at West Point, New York; Has final argument with John Allan.

1831—Is court-martialed and dismissed from West Point; Publishes *Poems* in New York City and returns to Baltimore to live with the Clemms; Unsuccessfully submits stories in a magazine story contest.

1833—His story "MS. Found in a Bottle" wins another magazine story contest.

1835—Joins the staff of the *Southern Literary Messenger* in Richmond; Brings Virginia and Maria Clemm to Richmond; Becomes editor of the *Southern Literary Messenger.*

1836—Marries teenage Virginia Clemm on May 16; Loses job because of drinking in December.

1837—Moves to New York City and finishes writing a novel, *The Narrative of Arthur Gordon Pym.*

1838—Moves to Philadelphia, Pennsylvania, and barely earns a living as a freelance writer.

1839—Becomes editor at *Burton's Gentleman's Magazine.*

1840—Quits *Burton's*; Publishes *Tales of the Grotesque and Arabesque.*

1841—Becomes editor at *Graham's Magazine*; Publishes his first detective story, "The Murders in the Rue Morgue."

1842—Virginia Poe breaks blood vessel in her throat on January 20; Poe learns she has tuberculosis; Quits his job at *Graham's* in April; Writes a number of brilliant, original stories, such as "The Mystery of

Marie Roget," "The Masque of the Red Death," "The Pit and the Pendulum," and "The Tell-Tale Heart;" Unsuccessfully tries to get a government job and to establish his own literary magazine, *The Stylus*.

1843—Writes stories "The Gold Bug" and "The Black Cat;" Gives a talk on "Poetry in America" during a lecture tour.

1844—Moves to New York City; Writes "The Balloon Hoax;" Goes to work for the New York *Mirror* newspaper.

1845—In January, publishes "The Raven" in the New York *Evening Mirror* newspaper; In February, becomes a partner at *The Broadway Journal* newspaper; Publishes two books: *Tales* and *The Raven and Other Poems*; In December, *The Broadway Journal* goes out of business.

1846—Moves to Fordham, New York; Conducts literary feud with writer Thomas Dunn English; Writes story "The Cask of Amontillado."

1847—Is grief-stricken when wife, Virginia, dies on January 30; Unsuccessfully attempts a romantic relationship with Marie Louise Shew; Writes a long essay called *Eureka*; Publishes poem "Ulalume" in December.

1848—Gives lecture in Lowell, Massachusetts; Falls in love with Nancy "Annie" Richmond, a married woman; Also declares love for Sarah Helen Whitman, a Providence, Rhode Island, poet; In November, attempts suicide in Boston; Becomes engaged to Whitman soon after; Due to Poe's drinking, wedding is called off by Whitman in December.

1849—Writes poem "Annabel Lee;" Is offered an opportunity to establish his literary magazine *The Stylus*; Travels to Richmond in June to raise money for the magazine by lecturing; Declares love to childhood sweetheart Elmira Royster Shelton; She agrees to marry him; Sets out for New York City to settle affairs on September 27; Is discovered sick on a Baltimore sidewalk on October 3; Dies at Washington College Hospital in Baltimore on October 7.

CHAPTER NOTES

Chapter 1. The Man in the Gutter

1. John Evangelist Walsh, *Midnight Dreary* (New Brunswick, N.J.: Rutgers University Press, 1998), p. 46.

2. Ibid., p. 42.

3. Arthur Hobson Quinn, *Edgar Allan Poe: A Critical Biography* (Baltimore: The Johns Hopkins University Press, 1998), p. 640.

4. William Bittner, *Poe* (Boston: Little, Brown and Company, 1962), p. 8.

5. Ibid., p. 7.

Chapter 2. The Orphan Boy

1. Bettina L. Knapp, *Edgar Allan Poe* (New York: Frederick Ungar Publishing Co., 1984), p. 9.

2. Ibid., p. 12.

3. Diane Johnson, "Dreams of E. A. Poe," *New York Review of Books*, July 18, 1991, p. 7.

4. Arthur Hobson Quinn, *Edgar Allan Poe: A Critical Biography* (Baltimore: The Johns Hopkins University Press, 1998), pp. 70–71.

5. Ibid., p. 82.

6. Ibid., p. 83.

7. Sara Sigourney Rice, *Edgar Allan Poe: A Memorial Volume* (Baltimore: Turnbull Brothers, 1877), p. 38.

8. Ibid., p. 6.

9. Ibid., p. 41.

10. Jeffrey Meyers, *Edgar Allan Poe: His Life and Legacy* (New York: Charles Scribner's Sons, 1992), p. 19.

11. Bittner, p. 36.

12. Quinn, p. 91.

Chapter 3. Scholar, Soldier, Poet, Story Writer

1. Jeffrey Meyers, *Edgar Allan Poe: His Life and Legacy* (New York: Charles Scribner's Sons, 1992), p. 24.

2. Ibid., p. 27.

3. Bettina L. Knapp, *Edgar Allan Poe* (New York: Frederick Ungar Publishing Co., 1984), p. 18.

4. Ibid.

5. John Taylor, "So Rare," *New York*, April 18, 1988, p. 67.

6. Meyers, p. 36.

7. Julian Symons, *The Tell-Tale Heart* (New York: Harper & Row, Publishers, 1978), p. 34.

8. Vincent Starrett, "A Poe Mystery Uncovered," *The Saturday Review of Literature*, May 1, 1943, p. 4.

9. Tom Johnson, "Cadet Edgar Allan Poe," *American Heritage*, June 1976, p. 62.

10. Ibid., p. 63.

11. Arthur Hobson Quinn, *Edgar Allan Poe: A Critical Biography* (Baltimore: The Johns Hopkins University Press, 1998), p. 166.

12. Johnson, p. 87.

13. Ibid.

14. Symons, p. 41.

15. Johnson, p. 88.

16. Symons, p. 41.

17. Wolf Mankowitz, *The Extraordinary Mr Poe* (New York: Summit Books, 1978), p. 88.

18. Sara Sigourney Rice, *Edgar Allan Poe: A Memorial Volume* (Baltimore: Turnbull Brothers, 1877), p. 60.

19. Mankowitz, p. 98.

Chapter 4. Editor of the *Southern Literary Messenger*

1. Arthur Hobson Quinn, *Edgar Allan Poe: A Critical Biography* (Baltimore: The Johns Hopkins University Press, 1998), pp. 219, 224.

2. James A. Harrison, ed., *The Complete Works of Edgar Allan Poe, Poe and His Friends: Letters Relating to Poe* (New York: AMS Press Inc., 1965), vol. 17, p. 21.

3. Jeffrey Meyers, *Edgar Allan Poe: His Life and Legacy* (New York: Charles Scribner's Sons, 1992), p. 84.

4. Sara Sigourney Rice, *Edgar Allan Poe: A Memorial Volume* (Baltimore: Turnbull Brothers, 1877), p. 61.

5. Meyers, p. 74.

6. Bettina L. Knapp, *Edgar Allan Poe* (New York: Frederick Ungar Publishing Co., 1984), p. 27.

7. Meyers, p. 82.

8. William Bittner, *Poe* (Boston: Little, Brown and Company, 1962), p. 112.

9. Meyers, p. 225.

10. Ibid., p. 91.

Chapter 5. In New York and Philadelphia, 1838–1841

1. *Works of Edgar Allan Poe* (New York: Gramercy Books, 1985), p. 589.

2. Jeffrey Meyers, *Edgar Allan Poe: His Life and Legacy* (New York: Charles Scribner's Sons, 1992), p. 93.

3. Stephan Jay Gould, "Poe's Greatest Hit," *Natural History*, July 1993, p. 14.

4. Ibid., p. 17.

5. William Bittner, *Poe* (Boston: Little, Brown and Company, 1962), p. 163.

6. Dr. Crypton, "The Ciphers of Edgar Allan Poe," *Science Digest*, October 1984, p. 62.

7. *Works of Edgar Allan Poe*, p. 245.

Chapter 6. Editor of *Graham's Magazine*

1. Julian Symons, *The Tell-Tale Heart* (New York: Harper & Row, Publishers, 1978), p. 71.

2. Edgar A. Poe, "A Chapter on Autobiography," *American Heritage*, February 1975, p. 99.

3. Ibid.

4. Ibid., p. 101.

5. Jeffrey Meyers, *Edgar Allan Poe: His Life and Legacy* (New York: Charles Scribner's Sons, 1992), p. 128.

6. Wolf Mankowitz, *The Extraordinary Mr Poe* (New York: Summit Books, 1978), p. 141.

7. William Bittner, *Poe* (Boston: Little, Brown and Company, 1962), pp. 177–178.

8. James A. Harrison, ed., *The Complete Works of Edgar Allan Poe, Poe and His Friends: Letters Relating to Poe* (New York: AMS Press Inc., 1965), vol. 17, p. 107.

Chapter 7. Freelance Writer

1. *Works of Edgar Allan Poe* (New York: Gramercy Books, 1985), p. 354.

2. Julian Symons, *The Tell-Tale Heart* (New York: Harper & Row, Publishers, 1978), p. 75.

3. William Bittner, *Poe* (Boston: Little, Brown and Company, 1962), p. 181.

4. Jeffrey Meyers, *Edgar Allan Poe: His Life and Legacy* (New York: Charles Scribner's Sons, 1992), p. 147.

5. Arthur Hobson Quinn, *Edgar Allan Poe: A Critical Biography* (Baltimore: The Johns Hopkins University Press, 1998), p. 371.

6. Wolf Mankowitz, *The Extraordinary Mr Poe* (New York: Summit Books, 1978), p. 148.

7. Bittner, p. 184.

8. Ibid.

9. Mankowitz, p. 163.

10. *Works of Edgar Allan Poe*, p. 382.

11. Meyers, p. 148.

12. Symons, p. 88.

13. Mankowitz, p. 173.

14. Meyers, p. 154.

15. Symons, p. 93.

Chapter 8. The Raven

1. *Works of Edgar Allan Poe* (New York: Gramercy Books, 1985), p. 707.

2. Jeffrey Meyers, *Edgar Allan Poe: His Life and Legacy* (New York: Charles Scribner's Sons, 1992), p. 164.

3. Sara Sigourney Rice, *Edgar Allan Poe: A Memorial Volume* (Baltimore: Turnbull Brothers, 1877), p. 24.

4. William Bittner, *Poe* (Boston: Little, Brown and Company, 1962), p. 208.

5. Arthur Hobson Quinn, *Edgar Allan Poe: A Critical Biography* (New York: Cooper Square Publishers, Inc., 1969), p. 461.

6. Ibid., p. 187.

7. Julian Symons, *The Tell-Tale Heart* (New York: Harper & Row, Publishers, 1978), p. 108.

8. Bittner, p. 211.

9. Ibid., p. 218.

10. Meyers, p. 196.

11. Meyers, pp. 204–205.

12. Ibid., p. 202.

13. *Works of Edgar Allan Poe*, p. 721.

14. Ibid., p. 207.

15. Mankowitz, p. 208.

Chapter 9. Last Days of the Raven

1. Hardin Craig, "Truth About Poe," *The Virginia Quarterly Review*, Spring 1942, p. 286.

2. Jeffrey Meyers, *Edgar Allan Poe: His Life and Legacy* (New York: Charles Scribner's Sons, 1992), p. 224.

3. Ibid., p. 213.

4. William Bittner, *Poe* (Boston: Little, Brown and Company, 1962), p. vii.

5. Meyers, p. 218.

6. Ibid., p. 219.

7. Julian Symons, *The Tell-Tale Heart* (New York: Harper & Row, Publishers, 1978), p. 134.

8. Bittner, p. 243.

9. Symons, pp. 136–137.

10. Philip Van Doren Stern, ed., *The Portable Edgar Allan Poe* (New York: Penguin Books, 1945), p. 574.

11. Meyers, pp. 235–236, 237.

12. Wolf Mankowitz, *The Extraordinary Mr Poe* (New York: Summit Books, 1978), p. 229.

13. Bittner, p. 257.

14. *Works of Edgar Allan Poe* (New York: Gramercy Books, 1985), p. 713.

15. Mankowitz, p. 232.

16. Bittner, p. 261.

17. Clifford Dowdey, "Poe's Last Visit to Richmond," *American Heritage*, April 1956, p. 25.

18. John Evangelist Walsh, *Midnight Dreary* (New Brunswick, N.J.: Rutgers University Press, 1998), p. 19.

19. Ibid., pp. 15–16.

20. Ibid., p. 24.

21. Meyers, p. 251.

22. Bittner, pp. 280–281.

23. Walsh, pp. 34–35.

24. Ibid., p. x.

25. Edmund Wilson, "Poe As a Literary Critic," *The Nation*, October 31, 1942, p. 452.

26. Mankowitz, p. 229.

GLOSSARY

acquaint—To cause to know personally.

ambition—A desire for success.

anatomical—Having to do with the structure of the body.

anonymously—Without being identified by name.

artillery—Cannons or other big guns.

biology—The science of plant and animal life.

bounty—A reward or bonus.

cholera—A deadly bacterial disease that affects the stomach and intestines.

constrain—To force.

delirious—In a condition of serious mental confusion.

derange—To make insane.

diabetes—A disease often caused by too much sugar in the blood.

dilemma—A problem or argument with two or more possible solutions.

entrance—To carry away with delight or wonder; to put into a trance.

heiress—A female who inherits property.

hieroglyphics—A system of picture writing.

hoax—A trick in which something fake is passed off as true.

intoxicated—Affected by alcohol.

linen—A cloth made from the fibers of the flax plant.

literary—Relating to the study of books or writing.

lyceum—A hall for public lectures, discussions, or entertainment.

manuscript—Handwritten pages.

melancholy—A condition of moodiness or depression.

molasses—A syrup made from raw sugar.

poverty—A condition of poorness or want.

preface—An author's remarks at the start of a piece of writing; an introduction.

principle—A rule, law, or code of conduct.

quartermaster—A military officer who provides food and clothing.

rabies—A disease of the nervous system caused by the bite of a rabid animal.

revise—To improve or correct.

sober—Not drunk.

subscribe—To pledge money or to agree to purchase.

unparalleled—Having no equal.

whirlpool—Water moving rapidly in a circle, causing a depression in the center into which floating objects may be drawn.

FURTHER READING

Anderson, Madelyn K. *Edgar Allan Poe, a Mystery*. Danbury, Conn.: Franklin Watts, Inc., 1993.

Hughes, Libby. *West Point*. Parsippany, N.J.: Silver Burdett Press, 1997.

Longfellow, Henry Wadsworth. *Selected Poems*, ed. Lawrence Buell. New York: Viking Penguin, 1988.

Meyers, Jeffrey. *Edgar Allan Poe: His Life and Legacy*. New York: Charles Scribner's Sons, 1992.

Poe, Edgar Allan. *Eight Tales of Terror*. New York: Scholastic, Inc., 1961.

———. *The Portable Edgar Allan Poe*, ed. Philip Van Doren Stern. New York: Penguin Books, 1985.

———. *The Tell-Tale Heart & Other Writings*. New York: Bantam Books, 1983.

Symons, Julian. *The Tell-Tale Heart*. New York: Harper & Row, Publishers, 1978.

INTERNET
ADDRESSES

Dauphin County Library System. *Cybertour: Edgar Allan Poe*. January 2000. <http://dcls.org/x/archives/poe.html>.

The Edgar Allan Poe Society of Baltimore. September 4, 2000. <http://www.eapoe.org/>.

National Park Service. *Edgar Allan Poe National Historic Site*. November 30, 2000. <http://www.nps.gov/edal/>.

The Poe Decoder. March 5, 2000. <http://www.poedecoder.com/>.

The Poe Museum. 1997. <http://www.poemuseum.org/>.

The Works of Edgar Allan Poe. 1996–1997. <http://www.pambytes.com/poe/poe.html>.

INDEX

DATE			